Textile Art of Japan

Sunny Yang   Rochelle M. Narasin

Textile

Art of Japan

Sunny Yang
Rochelle M. Narasin

SHUFUNOTOMO/JAPAN PUBLICATIONS

To my mother, who opened my eyes
to appreciate the beauty of the world,
and to my husband, Insuk Yang
...to whom I owe so much. — S. Yang

To Bruce, Ben, and Lisa. — R. M. Narasin

First printing, 1989

Book Design by Toshiaki Suzuki

Published by Shufunotomo. Co., Ltd.,
2-9, Kanda Surugadai, Chiyoda-ku,
Tokyo, 101 Japan

DISTRIBUTORS
United States: Kodansha International/USA, Ltd.
through Farrar, Straus & Giroux,
19 Union Square West, New York 10003.
Canada: Fitzhenry & Whiteside Ltd.,
195 Allstate Parkway, Markham, Ontario L3R 4T8.
European Continent: European Book Service PBD,
Strijkviertel 63, 3454 PK De Meern, The Netherlands.
Australia and New Zealand: Bookwise International,
54 Crittenden Road, Findon, South Australia 5023.
The Far East: Japan Publications Trading Co.,
1-2-1, Sarugaku-cho, Chiyoda-ku, Tokyo 101.

Printed in Japan

ISBN 0-87040-773-2

Foreword

In each culture around the world, food, clothing, and shelter—those foundations of human life—are the natural expressions and symbols of that culture.

Though the kimono is the Japanese national costume, it functions in the same way as the costumes of other cultures. It protects the body, it decorates it, and it expresses social status. When people from other cultures see the kimono as being unique or different from any other national costume it is not the function of the kimono that they are referring to but to the particular forms those functions take in the kimono.

The Japanese kimono, like the clothing of other cultures, was woven from vegetable or animal fibers. At present, of course, most kimono are made from manmade fibers. In Japan, the main fibers have been hemp and silk. The same is true of China and Korea. In the fifteenth century, with the growth of cotton production in China, the techniques of cotton spinning and weaving were introduced to Japan, and cotton fabric became widely used throughout the nation. In contrast, the main sources of fiber in Europe were flax and wool. This difference is simply a difference of the physical environments of the two cultural spheres.

In Japan, the main methods of weaving have been flat weave, twill weave, satin weave, gauze weaves, and tapestry-style weaves, techniques which are used around the world.

Vegetable dyes have been widely used in Japan, among them indigo and safflower. In Europe vegetable dyes were also used, including indigo and madder. From the seventeenth century, Europeans imported tropical plants from South America and created bright and colorful dyes from them; in the same fashion, the Japanese derived bright colors from the plant materials they imported from the jungles of Southeast Asia and India. Of course today both Japan and Europe use manmade dyes. In other words, the basic techniques of textile production are universal.

The original model for the Japanese kimono, which has undergone many changes in its form from the eighth century, was the official costume of the Chinese nobility and scholar-bureaucrats. It was a long robe in a single piece. But the common people in China, who had to work, converted that costume into a two-piece garment that provided more mobility. In Japan as well, the working classes traditionally wore a two-piece garment, and even when Westernization increased greatly in the second half of the nineteenth century, the traditional form of workers' clothing remained largely unchanged.

How is it, then, that the kimono, which developed on the basis of universal techniques and trends of textile production, is able to be an expression of a particular and unique culture? Because the color and design of kimono patterns are the products of two specifically Japanese factors: the function of the kimono in Japanese society and the tradition of Japanese aesthetics. The universal functions of the kimono are given specific expression and form by the particular characteristics of Japanese culture.

The Japanese regard color as something that changes with time rather than as an eternal, unchanging thing. The Japanese words for colors, such as *sakura iro* (cherry-blossom color) and *momiji iro* (maple-leaf color) are broad descriptions instead of true definitions of colors.

There are many different colors of cherry blossoms, and many different shades of color in maple leaves. An extremely broad range of light pinks is called "cherry blossom" by the Japanese. Similarly, some seven to eight different shades of indigo are differentiated, from the lightest (*kamenozoki*, literally, a peek in the dye vat), to the deepest (*shimbashi*). And each of those shades, too, changes over time. Color is not a fixed entity but something that changes ceaselessly. The colors that have decorated the kimono were conceived within this view of color.

Next are pattern and design. China has been a pioneer in weaving techniques to produce various textile designs, and Japan imported those techniques in the eighth century. In addition, applying designs on kimonos with dyes and pigments became extremely popular from the tenth century.

Applying designs to kimono was a way of emphasizing the uniqueness of its wearer. Based on this way of thinking, Japanese drew not only on the natural world but on the enormous variety of manmade objects as sources for kimono designs. In the eighteenth century, the tools and appliances of everyday life became motifs in kimono designs.

In addition, scenes and sentiments from Japanese poetry and from Chinese literature were also widely adopted. The virtues of the Chinese philosophy of Confucianism, too, were depicted in a symbolic manner, and they are still popular today—the auspicious design motif of pine, bamboo, and plum (*sho chiku bai*) is not simply a plant motif. It is a symbolic representation of the Confucian virtues. In European dress, individuality and uniqueness were sought in the cut and shape of clothing, but in Japan it was color and design that made each kimono a unique work of art, and bestowed distinction and individuality on each person wearing one.

Mitsukuni Yoshida
Honorary Professor of Kyoto University

Preface

Although we were aware of the elegant kimono with its vibrant colors and exotic motifs, we were especially struck by the beauty of Japanese hand-dyed and woven fabrics when we arrived in Japan about four years ago. We felt that these fabrics were special forms of art. We became extremely interested in learning who created these fibers and fabrics, what techniques they used, what meaning their design motifs had, and what significance the different fabrics had to Japanese in different places and different times.

We found that while there were a few good books in English that treated textiles and related subjects in depth, there was not an introductory book that answered the general questions we had. To satisfy our curiosity, we began to research and collect information about history, motifs, and techniques used to create Japanese fabrics. This book is the result: a combination of relatively simple explanations illustrated with fine examples of the various kinds of Japanese textiles.

Handcrafted textiles are increasingly being replaced by mass-produced bolts of fabrics. In Japan, there is a small number of artists and craftsmen striving to maintain a dying tradition by using age-old methods, refining them, and contributing to the fabrics used in contemporary Japanese life. In an attempt to show a glimpse into what may be possible, we have included some alternative uses of fabrics devised by today's innovative people.

In the process of collecting data, we have had a wonderful experience, both enjoyable and educational, meeting with all those who were eager to provide us with the materials we have used in this book. We sincerely appreciate their help. We are especially grateful to Kuniko Kishimoto, Miwako Kimura, and the staffs of the museums for their advice on sources of information; Anna Esaki and Kathryn Lohr for their help with the first draft of our manuscript; Isamu Machida for the beautiful photographs; Shunichi Kamiya, our editor at Shufunotomo, for his guidance and immense patience; and all our friends and our husbands and children for their constant encouragement and support, which made this project possible.

Major Textile-Producing Areas of Japan

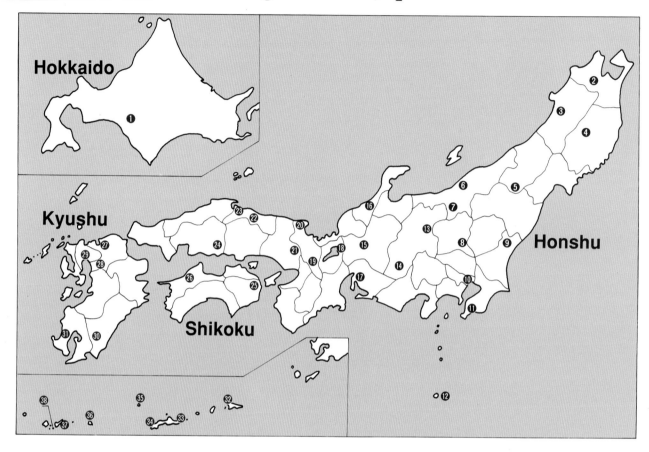

Places (Prefectures) / Names of Products

1. **Hiratori** (Hokkaido) / *Atsushi ori.*
2. **Hirosaki** (Aomori) / Tsugaru *kogin.*
3. **Akita** (Akita) / Akita *hachijo.*
4. **Morioka** (Iwate) / Nambu *tsumugi*, Nambu *sikon-zome.*
5. **Yonezawa** (Yamagata) / Yonezawa *tsumugi*, *benibana-zome, oitama tsumugi.*
6. **Ojiya** (Niigata) / Ojiya *chijimi*, Ojiya *tsumugi*, Echigo *jofu.*
7. **Tokamachi** (Niigata) / Echigo *jofu.*
8. **Kiryu** (Gunma) / *Omeshi chirimen.*
9. **Yuki** (Ibaraki) / Yuki *tsumugi.*
10. **Tokyo** (Tokyo) / Edo *yuzen*, Edo *komon.*
11. **Tateyama** (Chiba) / *Tozan ori.*
12. **Hachijo Island** (Tokyo) / *Kihachijo.*
13. **Ueda** (Nagano) / Ueda *tsumugi.*
14. **Iida** (Nagano) / Shinshu Iida *tsumugi.*
15. **Gujo Hachiman** (Gifu) / Gujo *tsumugi.*
16. **Kanazawa** (Ishikawa) / Kaga *yuzen.*
17. **Arimatsu, Narumi** (Aichi) / *Shibori.*
18. **Nagahama** (Shiga) / Nagahama *chirimen.*
19. **Kyoto** (Kyoto) / Kyo *yuzen*, Kyo *kanoko shibori*, *kinran, kara ori, tsuzure ori.*
20. **Mineyama** (Kyoto) / Tango *chirimen.*
21. **Sasayama** (Hyogo) / Tamba *momen.*
22. **Kurayoshi** (Tottori) / Kurayoshi *gasuri.*
23. **Sakaiminato** (Tottori) / Yumihama *gasuri.*
24. **Fuchu** (Hiroshima) / Bingo *gasuri.*
25. **Tokushima** (Tokushima) / *Aizome.*
26. **Matsuyama** (Ehime) / Iyo *gasuri.*
27. **Hakata** (Fukuoka) / Hakata obi.
28. **Kurume** (Fukuoka) / Kurume *gasuri.*
29. **Saga** (Saga) / Saga *nishiki.*
30. **Miyakonojo** (Miyazaki) / Satsuma *tsumugi.*
31. **Kagoshima** (Kagoshima) / Oshima *tsumugi.*
32. **Amami Oshima Island** (Kagoshima) / Oshima tsumugi.
33. **Kijoka** (Okinawa) / *Bashofu*
34. **Naha** (Okinawa) / *Bingata*, Ryukyu *gasruri.*
35. **Kume Island** (Okinawa) / Kumejima *gasuri.*
36. **Miyako Island** (Okinawa) / Miyako *jofu*, Miyako *gasuri.*
37. **Ishigaki Island** (Okinawa) / Yaeyama *jofu.*
38. **Taketomi Island** (Okinawa) / *Bashofu, Minsa ori.*

1

The History
of the Kimono

Noh costume. Motifs of eight-arched bridge, paper poem strips, flowers, and grasses in embroidery and gold-leaf imprint on a silk red-and-white block design (*dangawari*) background. Momoyama period. Tokyo National Museum.

The wearing of the kimono is both a state of mind and a state of dress. Grace and serenity accompany its presence and the beauty it evokes in our minds leaves a lasting image of the essence of Japan, while imprinting its elegant silhouette on our memories.

The silk kimono, a highly prized heirloom, is passed down from generation to generation, its unchanging style retaining its beauty from year to year. Great care is taken in choosing the fabric from which it is made. The size and style of the motif, as well as the quality and color of the fabric, indicate the age, status, and taste of its owner. Bright colors and large motifs are worn by young girls. Their long-sleeved kimono (*furisode*) provide a great contrast with the subdued colors and smaller decorations of a married woman's short-sleeved kimono (*kosode*).

The kimono has a long history, reflecting influences felt from the cultures of India, China, Korea, and Southeast Asia. While the early textile history of Japan is misty, archaeologists have determined that prior to 300 B.C., wood or vegetable fibers were used to make fabrics which were fashioned into belted two-piece garments. There is also evidence that silk was used in western Japan as early as the fourth century. Signaling the advent of Japan's written history, the Asuka period (sixth century) brought trade between Japan and two of its neighbors, China and Korea. From these exchanges came two valuable imports: clothing from China, including the basic kimono form; and the Buddhist religion—which had tremendous influence on Japanese art and textiles—from Korea. The continuation of this exchange with China during the next two centuries brought elaborate textiles to Japan in the Nara period (seventh and eighth centuries).

Kyoto was the capital of Japan during the Heian period, which spanned the eighth through twelfth centuries. The aristocrats whose culture flourished in that era took a great interest in clothing. The *junihitoe* (twelve unlined robes), the official costume of the noble ladies of the day, consisted of from twelve to up to twenty layers of robes of different colors. The robes were worn so that a narrow band of each was visible at the neck, sleeves, and hem, and great importance was attached to the effect of the color combinations.

In the twelfth century, the aristocratic Heian culture declined and the samurai warrior class assumed control of the government. They transferred the political capital to Kamakura in eastern Japan and placed restrictions on dress to control its extravagance. For themselves, they chose the practical clothing of the commoners, as it was more convenient to wear in battle and coincided with the simplicity of the warrior life they followed. The ladies discarded the uncomfortable and bulky *junihitoe* and adopted the simple *kosode* and *hakama*, which had been the undergarment of Kyoto's court ladies and

Junihitoe worn in the Heian period. Tokyo National Museum.

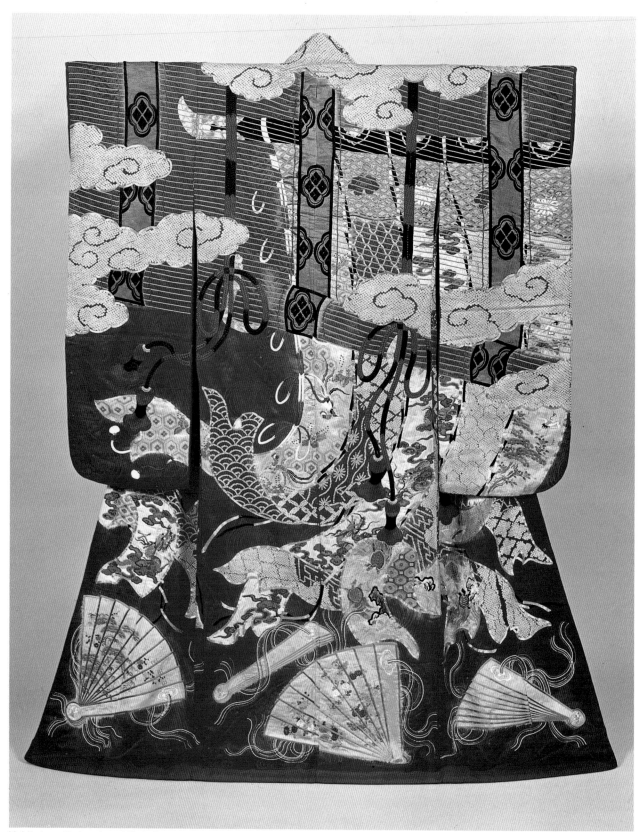

Uchikake with bamboo blind, fans, and cloth screen (*kicho*). Tie-dye clouds divide the typical Genroku-era design. Edo period. National Museum of Japanese History.

the basic outer garment of the commoners.

It is from the *kosode* that the present form of the kimono developed. This practical garment, closed only with a sash called an obi, fit everyone. It was made from a piece of fabric nine yards long and fifteen inches wide. The fabric was cut into rectangular pieces of a predetermined length, selvages intact, and stitched into the basic kimono form. Initially, the plainness of this garment was relieved by the addition of an elaborately decorated outer robe, the *uchikake*. But as time went by, the desire for more decorative *kosode* emerged, and new and more elaborate techniques for decorating textiles, such as *shibori* (tie-dye) and gold- and silver-leaf imprint techniques (*surihaku*), were developed.

In the middle of the fourteenth century, a new line of shoguns, the Ashikaga family, abolished the Kamakura shogunate and returned the capital to Kyoto. The Ashikaga rulers were men of cultivated taste and fervid patrons of the arts. Their rule is known as the Muromachi period (1338–1568) after the Muromachi district in Kyoto, where the third Ashikaga shogun Yoshimitsu built his palace. Yoshimitsu is also known as the builder of the Golden Pavilion, Kinkakuji, where he planned to retire and live as a Buddhist monk. During this period, Zen Buddhism strongly influenced the arts. Not only did ink painting reach a new height, but the Noh drama, supported by the shoguns, developed from an agricultural festival dance to a highly refined dramatic art. The Muromachi period was paradoxical in many ways: it was characterized by domestic unrest and civil war on one hand and prosperity, cultural development, and the resumption of trade with China under the Ming dynasty (1368–ca. 1644) on the other. Japanese merchants became wealthy, and as the living standard rose, they demanded more elaborate clothing, leading to the development of even more ornate textiles. It was during this

period that *tsujigahana* (stitched tie-dye combined with ink painting, gold- or silver-leaf imprint embellishments, and embroidery on silk) began to evolve.

Another important development in the field of textiles at this time was the import of cotton from Korea and China in the fifteenth century. The plant flourished in Japan and was valued because it provided greater warmth, and was easier and cheaper to raise, process, and dye than the bast fibers used up to that time.

Fan, flower, and bamboo motifs in embroidery, gold-leaf imprint, tie-dye, and divided dyeing. Mounted on a folding screen. Momoyama period. National Museum of Japanese History.

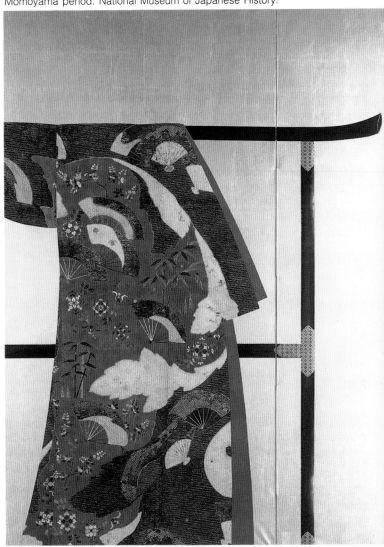

The Momoyama period (1568–1600) saw the unification of Japan under the warlord Oda Nobunaga. Nobunaga was assassinated in 1582, and power passed to his leading vassal, Toyotomi Hideyoshi, who continued to consolidate the country. Hideyoshi's death was followed by a seventeen-year struggle between his heirs and a rival general, Tokugawa Ieyasu, in which Ieyasu finally triumphed. In this brief period, artists and artisans were called upon to perform to the highest level of their ability.

During the Momoyama period, the art of *tsujigahana* reached the zenith of its short existence. Some of the most beautiful kimono ever created were made using this combination of techniques, but *tsujigahana* fell victim to the complexity that made it so special, and it disappeared as an art form during the sixteenth century. Along with the demand for dyed masterpieces came the need for more elaborately woven fabrics, and in Kyoto, a special area of the city, Nishijin, was established as a weaving center.

After Ieyasu's triumph over the descendants of Hideyoshi, he moved the capital back to eastern Japan, to the village of Edo (now Tokyo), and the Edo period (1600–1868) began. His descendants ruled for more than two hundred years. During their reign they isolated Japan from any outside influences by prohibiting trade and cultural exchange with the rest of the world.

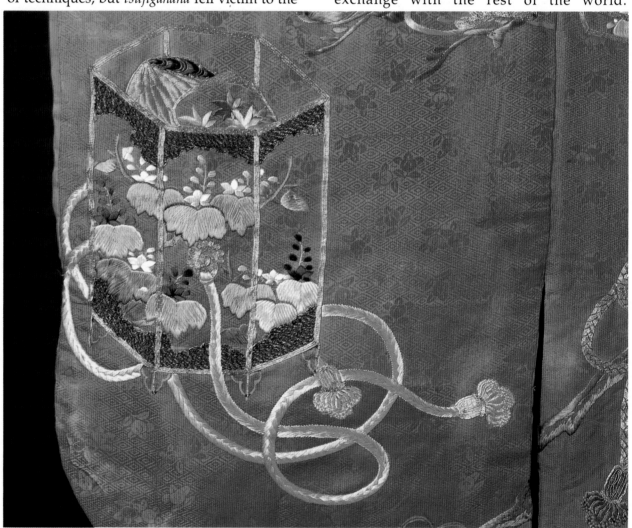

Sleeve of a *kosode* in scarlet silk *rinzu* (satin float patterned weave). Decorated with embroidery of paulownia and a small hexagonal chest of the sort used for storing the painted clamshells of an ancient shell-matching game. Edo period. Tokyo National Museum.

Kosode. Beautiful scenery on blue crepe *(chirimen)*, in *yuzen* and embroidery. The Uji Bridge is embellished with couched gold thread. Edo period. Tokyo National Museum.

Christianity, which had been introduced by Spanish and Portuguese missionaries in the sixteenth century, was banned entirely. Edo became a flourishing metropolis and attracted all sorts of merchants and artisans, eager to work and make their fortunes. While the peasants remained poor, the rich townsmen wanted to live well and enjoy the good things in life. They wanted entertainment, fine clothes, and beautiful possessions. To meet this demand, a wide variety of richly decorated textiles was created. Kimono decorated with brush painting, tie-dyeing techniques, embroidery, and gold and silver were in great demand and became very expensive. Though the government prohibited such extravagant dress again and again, the wealthy merchants in particular continued to buy lavish kimono and find ways to circumvent the laws.

With the availability of softer silks, artists began to see the kimono as a "canvas" to be painted. The versatility of the newly developing dyeing process called *yuzen*, in which the outlines of designs were drawn freehand, then painted in with dye and reserved with paste resist, allowed artists freedom to explore and expand their creativity and incorporate all the subtlety of the art of painting into kimono design. The woodblock prints of the period show many elegant and exotic motifs on kimono worn by the leading courtesans and famous Kabuki actors of the day. Artists such as Haranobu, Masanobu, Utamaro, Kiyonaga, and Kunisada not only recorded the vigorous, bold, and flamboyant tastes of the townsmen and women of Edo, but through the popularity of their prints, also influenced and stimulated kimono design.

The Meiji Restoration of 1868 returned power to the emperor, and the days of rule by the shogunate ended. The doors of Japan were open once more to the outside world, and cultural exchange resumed. The incoming Western influences changed Japanese social life and dress, in particular after World War II. Western clothing became more popular, though the traditional kimono remained acceptable for formal occasions. Many young people lost interest in carrying on traditional craft and textile techniques, and at the same time, mass production increased its reach into former handicraft areas, causing the decline of these traditions.

From the beginning of the twentieth century, the kimono and the craftsmen who create it have been slowly disappearing. Yet there is still a small group of artisans who continue to create beautiful textiles using traditional techniques combined with contemporary media and sensibilities. With their skills and imagination they are combining age-old processes with today's life style. We can only hope that this trend will stimulate and influence more people to rekindle the fire of innovation and creativity in order to expand the unique world of Japanese textile art.

Semiformal *yuzen* kimono.

From modest beginnings the obi has become the focal point of the kimono ensemble of today. Starting as the narrow sash that held up the culotte-like pants called *hakama*, it has evolved into an expensive and elaborate work of art. Whether woven of rich silk brocade, embroidered, or dyed, it is an essential part of the kimono, not only decoratively but functionally: since the kimono has no buttons or fasteners of any kind, it relies entirely on the obi to keep it closed.

In the Kamakura period, the obi was a back-tied bast fiber sash two or three inches wide, but during the Muromachi period it was sometimes made from silk. This slightly wider sash was decorated with plaids and checks in the Momoyama period, and its trailing ends were tucked in. It was during this time that the so-called Nagoya obi was created, when courtesans in the city of Nagoya copied the manner in which the Chinese artisans working in that city tied a cord around their waist several times.

It wasn't until the Edo period, when the obi's variety reached its height, that it became important in its own right and new ways of tying it were developed. Before that time, the kimono was the center of attention, but as fewer innovations developed in its decoration,

the weavers and dyers turned their attention to the obi and began making more elaborate, wider, and longer fabrics for it. In the 1670s it

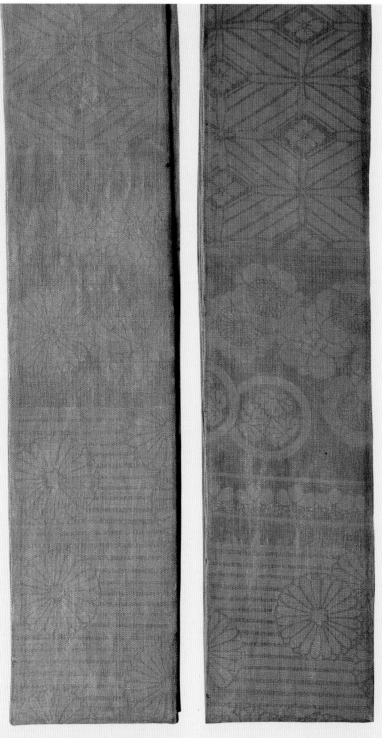

Woman's obi with woven grass and flower motifs and gold-leaf imprints on hemp. Momoyama period. Tokyo National Museum.

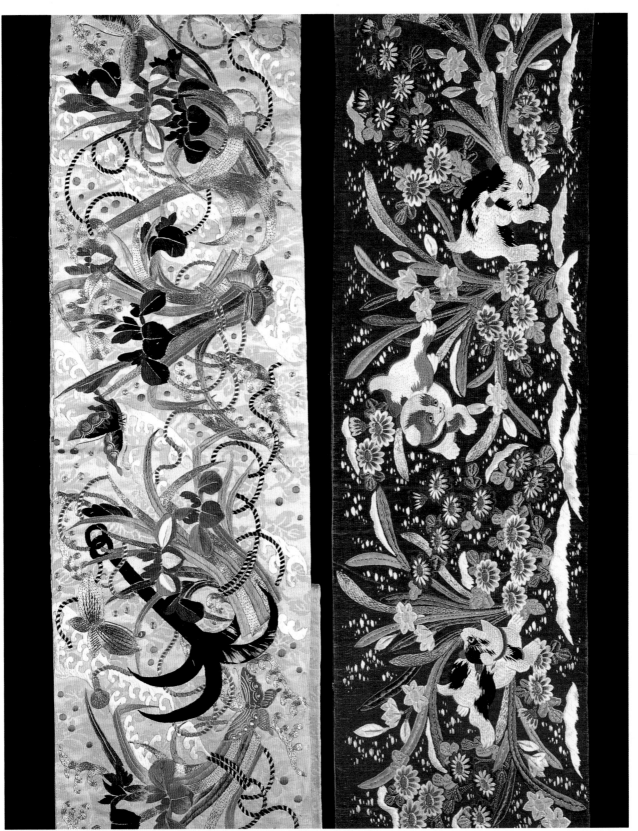

Left: woman's obi. All-over embroidery of butterflies, iris, and anchor motifs on white *donsu*.
Right: woman's obi. Embroidery of grass, flower, and puppies on red velvet. Edo period. Tokyo National Museum.

was from six to seven inches in width. The bow was variously placed on the side and at the front, but it moved to its permanent position in the back after an actor, imitating a young girl's fashion, wore an obi tied in back on stage and started a new style.

Today, formal and semiformal kimono are worn with specific types of obi. The double-width, fully patterned *maru* obi is the most formal and is made of heavy fabrics such as the multicolored patterned weave called *nishiki*, tapestry weave *(tsuzure ori)*, or gold brocade *(kinran)*. The formal double-fold *fukuro* obi, with its plain underside, is decorated over sixty percent of its front surface. The versatile, light-weight Nagoya obi, which can be used for a variety of occasions, is made of silk gauze damask or dyed gauze.

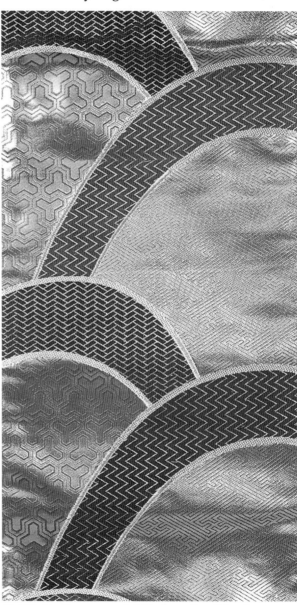

Tsuzure ori obi with motifs of cards used in an aristocratic pastime of the Heian-period, a contest in which participants tried to guess the contents of different kinds of incense that were burned. The auspicious motifs of pine, bamboo, and plum are woven designs.

Nishiki obi with many small, intricate motifs within a large wave design.

Kenjo (offering) Hakata obi woven by Zenzaburo Ogawa, a Living National Treasure.

Casual kimono and the unlined cotton kimono called *yukata* are worn with the unlined *(hitoe)* obi or the half-width *(hanhaba)* obi. Men's informal obi are usually soft silk, tied in a bow, while their formal obi are stiffer and narrower than women's obi.

While married women limit themselves to plain, flat bows, such as the drum bow *(taiko musubi)*, young girls may choose from a vast array of intricate tying styles. The tying of any obi bow is a complex maneuver. A brief summary of the steps involved may shed a little light on the process. The kimono is closed with the left side on top. Since the kimono is

Summer obi of *ro* weave in cool colors and designs.

Spring: This spring obi is of the style worn by women of the samurai class in the Edo period. Crepe with cherry blossoms dyed by the *yuzen* method and gold-leaf imprint.

Summer: Sailboats float on a rippling stream weaving between summer grasses, all depicted by the *yuzen* process against the pale background color of this light *ro* fabric, which contributes to the cool feeling appropriate to the season. Again, an obi for women of the samurai class.

Autumn: Pale blue-gray crepe fabric with a yellow and white chrysanthemums dyed in the *yuzen* process.

Winter: Deep pink crepe dyed with red and white camellias in the *yuzen* process.

longer than the person wearing it, a tuck is made at the waist and secured unobtrusively with a silk sash *(koshi himo)*. The obi is then tied around the wearer, with the kimono tuck in place and visible below it. At the back, two ends of the obi are left, one two feet long, the other four feet long. These ends are tied into a bow which is puffed out by a small pillow, all held together by the narrow silk cord *(obijime)* that is tied or fastened with the small *obidome* clasp. In the end, the obi becomes a functional ornament, for not only does it look lovely but its layers combine to form a pocket along its top rim in which to carry small objects. The formal obi is a work of art that is kept, treasured, and handed down from mother to daughter. It compares with expensive jewels in its monetary as well as sentimental value.

Braided *obijime* in striking colors.

Tie-dyed *obiage*, a scarflike piece of cloth tucked into the top of the obi to cover the *koshi himo*. Bright colors are used for young women.

Various types of *obidome*.

Semiformal. *Seigaiha* (ocean-wave style). This obi is a combination of *kara ori* and *shusu ori*.

Formal. For young women. *Tateya* (slanted arrow style). The scrolling plant motif called *karakusa* is executed in *nishiki ori*.

Formal. *Matsuba niju daiko* (pine-needle double-drum style). The Western-style flower and scrolling plant design is executed in *nishiki ori*.

Formal. For young women. *Fukurasuzume* (puffed sparrow style). The auspicious motif *noshi*—originally strips of dried abalone, but often artistically rendered, as here, as strips of fabric—depicted in *nishiki ori*.

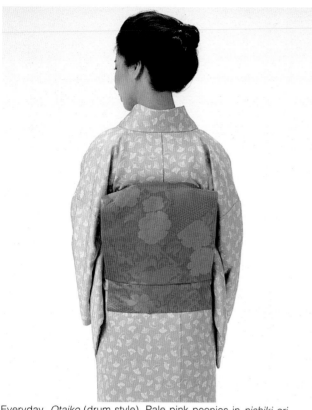

Everyday. *Otaiko* (drum style). Pale pink peonies in *nishiki ori.*

For a young woman's *yukata. Bunko musubi* (ribbon style) in half-width obi.

For men. *Kainokuchi* (shell-shape style). Hakata obi.

For men. *Katabasami* (one-end folded style) Hakata obi.

3

Dyed Textiles

Different dyeing techniques displayed on cloth wrappers (*furoshiki*) of silk crepe.

In Japan, there is no division between fine and decorative arts, and craftsmanship is very highly valued. The hands of many artists and craftsmen are still busily and beautifully decorating textiles in Japan, and dyeing is one of the processes they use most distinctively and creatively. From ancient times, people the world over have been dyeing textiles, and the process ranges from simply rubbing a leaf over woven fibers to the sophisticated techniques of tie-dyeing and *yuzen*. Whatever the technique, dyeing has offered nearly unlimited possibilities for self-expression, and these are marvelously exploited in Japanese textiles.

The variety of designs applied to fabrics in Japan is limitless. The names of most colors in Japanese are derived from their dye sources, and the colors themselves were seen as the essence of the "spirit" within the plant. When transferred to cloth, the spirit in the color would protect the garment's wearer. This belief may have come from the medicinal qualities possessed by many dye plants.

As elsewhere in the world, colors also signified social status, and certain colors were assigned to each of the court ranks. The color purple was placed highest because of its rarity, while abundant indigo was the lowest. Whatever the color, however, the dyeing process itself is extremely difficult, time-consuming, and fraught with possibilities for failure. Even for experienced professional dyers, the results of any dying process remain unpredictable. Unexpected bleeding of the colors, miscalculation of dye materials, unfavorable weather conditions, and the fact that most errors cannot be corrected once the dye has been applied to the fabric all plague the dyer, who must be very skillful, experienced, and well-trained to achieve pleasing results.

Until the middle of the nineteenth century, when chemical dyes were invented, dyes were extracted from natural substances. Crushed insects, charcoal soot, and ground minerals were all sources of dyes, but most dyes came from plants. Vegetable dyes are combined with mordants such as iron, ash lye, plum vinegar, or alum. These mordants, applied before or after dyeing, fix the color on the fabric and at the same time control the resulting hues. Several colors can be obtained from one dye source depending on the choice of the mordant. Vegetable dyes are still used today, though on a limited basis.

One of the most characteristic of Japanese dyes is indigo, or *ai*. Indigo was brought to Japan from China some time before the third century. At first it was applied to fabric by rubbing the leaves of the mountain indigo, *yama ai*, over material or by immersing the fabric in a dye solution made by soaking the cut leaves of the plant in water. By the Nara period, *yama ai* had been replaced by "buckwheat indigo," or *tade ai*, and the method of fermented dyeing used today had been mastered. From the Edo period, with the widespread cultivation of cotton, indigo-dyed fabric became an important product. Today, the number of traditional dyers has diminished, but fortunately the interest in natural dyes has not totally disappeared and indigo blue, in all its shades, is still very popular in Japan.

Another group of coloring agents, pigments, has been used to dye fabric in Okinawa and as fill-in color for small motifs on textiles on the mainland. These pigments, organic or inorganic, are combined with liquid soybean extract. They do not penetrate the fabric, but the protein in the soybean liquid hardens, bonding the pigment to the material.

Representative dyeing processes and techniques that have flourished over the years in Japanese textile history include tie-dyeing and paste-resist dyeing, both of which make extensive use of indigo dye, the first Japanese dye we will look at.

These color samples show the wide range of vegetable dyes that can be produced.

reasons, farmers began to plant cotton in place of rice, making it abundant and easily accessible. It was also believed that the ammonia in the indigo repelled mosquitoes and snakes, making indigo-dyed clothing perfect for farmers and field workers. With the availability of cotton and the practicality of the combination of it with indigo, indigo increased in popularity.

Indigo can be produced in a wide variety of shades, ranging from very pale to almost black. The depth of color is governed by either the strength of the dye into which the fibers are immersed or the number of times the fibers to be dyed are dipped in the indigo. The vat must be very strong when the fabric to be dyed is covered with paste, as it is in the paste-resist dyeing called *katazome*, because the paste cannot withstand lengthy exposure to moisture. But when dyeing yarn or thread for weaving, paste is not used, so the dye can be

Aizome
Indigo Dyeing

There is a certain mystique connected with indigo. Dyers revere it and pray to their god, Aizen Myoo, for good fortune in their work. They carefully tend the dye vat and give it the respect they would a friend. They stir it daily to keep it alive, and replenish it when necessary. Indigo is the principal dyeing substance they use to transform cotton, hemp cloth, ramie, and silk into rich blue masterpieces in a process called *aizome*.

When cotton was introduced to Japan in the fifteenth century, indigo had found its own best friend, for the two were perfectly matched. Indigo beautifully colored the fibers of this difficult-to-dye fabric, while at the same time it strengthened its fibers by building up in layers on them. Cotton was also much softer than the rough hemp fibers that had been available before its appearance. For these

Drying the indigo-dyed thread in the sun.

Stencil-dyed *furisode* with maple-leaf, cherry-blossom, pine-needle, and pine-cone motifs on an indigo background. Edo period. Tokyo National Museum.

weaker and the number of dips increased according to the depth of color desired. For these reasons, large hand-dyeing houses have vats of different strengths. They are sunk into the ground in sets of four. In the center of each group of four vats is a fire hole, which is lit when the weather turns cold in order to keep the indigo at the proper temperature for dyeing.

It is indigo that makes the beautiful blue of *yukata* fabric. Developed in the Genroku era (1688–1704), the *yukata* was first worn in the bath houses of Kyoto and Osaka, and soon was seen on the streets. The rich merchants of the Edo period, forbidden to wear silk, turned to the dyers for innovative ideas, and this popular item of clothing was developed. Especially favored by courtesans and men about town, its popularity increased until it reached a peak in the Meiji period.

Stencil-dyed indigo on cotton and ramie.

Indigo plants.

Using a bamboo rake to turn over the indigo leaves during the fermenting process to adjust the temperature.

Spreading water on the indigo leaves to provide the moisture that assists the fermenting process.

Indigo vats buried in the ground. The small holes are heat sources.

Checking the condition of the indigo in the vat.

Yukata fabric was originally dyed by applying paste to both sides of the fabric through a stencil before dyeing, but the process has been modernized. Today, a roll of fabric is stenciled with paste, sprinkled with sawdust, and folded. The dye is then applied to the fabric and pulled down through the layers of material with a vacuum. The paste is removed, and then the cloth is exposed to air. This exposure is essential in the process of indigo dyeing, because the oxygen in the air causes it to turn blue. The range of blue-and-white designs includes dots, checks, birds, flowers, landscapes, the scrolling plant motif known as *karakusa*, and small all-over designs *(komon)*.

Yukata fabric is used today for casual summer wear. Heavier cotton is used for farmers' clothes, the tradesman's half-length coat called a *hanten*, kimono-shaped stuffed bed covers *(yogi)*, square wrapping cloths *(furoshiki)*, quilt covers *(futonji)*, and decorative door curtains cum room dividers *(noren)*. The size of the pattern varies according to the size of the piece being made. Commercial *noren*, for instance, must be wide enough to cover the width of a door opening and adequately advertise the name of the shop. Their designs are usually large and simple, while *yukata* motifs can be small and very complex.

A style of indigo dyeing called *chayazome* is said to have been developed in Kyoto in the seventeenth century by a certain Chaya Sori, a feudal lord serving the Ashikaga clan who had learned this technique through trade with foreign countries. The Chayas eventually gave up their samurai status to become merchants, supplying the high-ranking ladies of the shogun's household with exquisite, elegant, and refined Chaya-dyed unlined summer kimono *(katabira)*.

Chayazome was done on a very high-quality light-weight pure white hemp. The fiber was grown near Nara and bleached and aged a full year before dyeing—always in a cool blue shade. A special technique was used to apply the resist paste to both sides of the fabric in all areas to be reserved from the dye, and the extremely detailed designs were done in indigo. The fine blue lines, regular and even in width throughout the entire length of fabric, stretch uninterrupted against the white background. *Chayazome* robes were perfect and luxurious summer wear: cool in color, light in weight, and usually decorated with refreshing designs of flowing streams or seashore scenes. Touches of gold couching and embroidery emphasized their luxury.

The different shades of indigo that can be obtained are clearly shown in these cotton *yukata*.

Chayazome katabira. Scenery dyed in indigo on white ramie, with gold embroidery. Edo period. National Museum of Japanese History.

Shibori

Tie-Dyeing

The origins of *shibori* are as hazy and mysterious as its soft, blurry designs. A form of resist dyeing, *shibori* was known before the advent of recorded history in countries around the world. In Japan, it was first documented in the Nara period. Textiles dyed by bound resist *(kokechi),* wax resist *(rokechi),* and carved wooden-block resist *(kyokechi)* were all imported from China and made domestically as well. Many fragments of these textiles are in the Shosoin Repository in Nara.

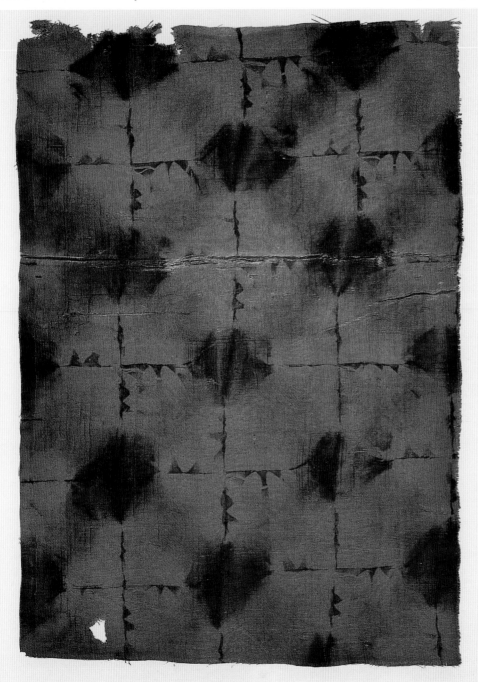

An example of fabric dyed with the *kokechi* technique of resist dyeing. Nara period. Tokyo National Museum

The Japanese word *shibori,* from the verb *shiboru,* to wring or squeeze, describes the dyeing process by which designs are created when the fabric is pinched, folded, gathered, knotted, tied, or pleated, and then bound tightly with a string to protect the fabric from the dye into which it is immersed. The results of this process are hazy patterns revealed when the bindings are removed: radial *(rasen),* squarish *(hitta),* short wood grain *(mokume),* or spider web *(kumo)* patterns appear. Hundreds of patterns can be created, depending on the method of tying and stitching.

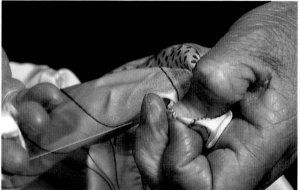
The tying process for *hitta shibori.*

Piles of cotton fabric after tying.

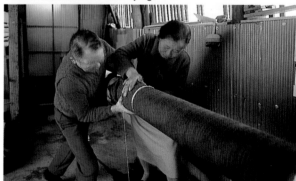
The *arashi* tying process requires more than one person. After wrapping the cloth tightly around the log, it is stitched and rolled up compactly, then dyed on the log.

Parrot motifs depicted using the *rokechi* technique of resist dyeing. Nara period. Tokyo National Museum.

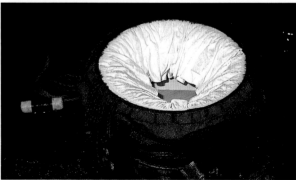
Oke (bucket) *shibori* just after the dyeing is completed. The cloth inside the wooden cylinder is reserved, and the portion sticking out after both lids are tyed on are dyed as the whole "bucket" is placed in the dye vat.

Two painted and tie-dyed *tsujigahana kosode* mounted on a folding screen. Momoyama periiod. National Museum of Japanese History.

In the Heian period, *shibori* was used to decorate banners and canopies for Buddhist religious ceremonies. Murasaki Shikibu, in her novel of Heian-period court life, *The Tale of Genji*, described elaborate costumes worn by the courtiers of the time, some of which were made of *shibori*-dyed material.

In the Kamakura period, the plain *kosode* that was worn at first by the women of the samurai class blossomed into vibrant and luxurious "fawn-spot tie-dye" *(kanoko shibori)* patterns. This Heian-period technique was accomplished by binding tiny bits of kimono

fabric. After dyeing the fabric, these bindings were removed, revealing small squarish or circular dots of undyed fabric in carefully planned designs.

At the same time, the surface of the *kosode* was being divided into large areas of color in a new form of design, divided dyeing *(somewake)*, which placed dyed areas in various configurations over the kimono. These dyed areas were sometimes arranged on the shoulder and hem, while at other times they were on either side of a vertical division. Another placement, called block-divided

Section of a *kosode*. Repeated patterns of maple leaves, deer, small flowers, and young pine branches arranged in diagonal bands on a black *rinzu* background. Edo period. Tokyo National Museum.

All-over fawn-spot tie-dye in ocean wave, fishnet, and peony motifs decorate this *furisode*. Edo period. Tokyo National Museum.

Paulownia and Japanese-style book motifs are delicately executed in tie-dye and embroidery on this *uchikake*. Edo period. National Museum of Japanese History.

dyeing *(dangawari)*, involved dividing the background into large squares of alternating colors.

The lack of control over the final effects inherent in the binding and dyeing process created many surprising designs. Craftsmen working in this medium soon found that by stitching shapes into the fabric and pulling them tight before dyeing, they had more control over the results. Not only could they make pictorial shapes, they could protect some areas with bamboo sheaths in order to have completely white areas, which they later embellished with ink and hand-applied colors. To this they added extra touches of gold- or silver-leaf imprint and embroidery. This combination of techniques—*tsujigahana*—developed throughout the turbulent Muromachi period and reached its height with the kimono worn by the nobility of the subsequent Momoyama period. It was one of Japan's finest contributions to textile art. The origin of the name of this uniquely Japanese form of dyeing remains a mystery. Whatever its origin, the robes created by this technique were admired enough to be owned, worn, and treasured by Tokugawa Ieyasu. It is because of his patronage that many still exist today, some designated Important Cultural Properties by the Japanese government. The end of *tsujigahana* as an art form opened the door for the development and subsequent popularity of all-over fawn-spot tie-dye, or *so kanoko*.

During the Edo period, feudal lords and their retainers passed through the town of Arimatsu in Aichi Prefecture on their way from Kyoto to Edo in order to comply with the Tokugawa shogunate's law mandating their presence in its new capital. They took advantage of the presence of a number of *shibori* shops and bought hand-dyed gifts during their stay in Arimatsu. Over the years, this small town's *shibori* industry grew and Arimatsu became the *shibori* center of Japan,

introducing several innovations to this dyeing process. Soon, the neighboring town, Narumi, joined Arimatsu in *shibori* production to meet the increasing demand. The dyers used cotton along with silk. Some shortcuts were developed to speed up the tedious process of hand-tying the material. A mechanical device called a *chikuwa* (a hook attached to a stand) was invented to hold the material during the tying process and *shibori* done by this method was called *chikuwa shibori*.

Simple and dynamic: the Japanese character for "ten" produced by tie-dyeing. Masako Shirasu collection.

Tradition with innovation. *Burning Sun*, an Itchiku *tsujigahana* work by the contemporary designer, Itchiku Kubota.

Today modern artists strive to preserve the ancient *shibori* technique while expanding its perspective and adding a contemporary excitement. One distinguished contemporary contributor is Itchiku Kubota. As a young man, he was mesmerized by a small piece of *tsujigahana* on exhibit at Tokyo National Museum. He spent years experimenting and developing his own method, which he calls Itchiku *tsujigahana*. He has succeeded in combining this traditional art with contemporary materials and techniques to create a form of expression all his own.

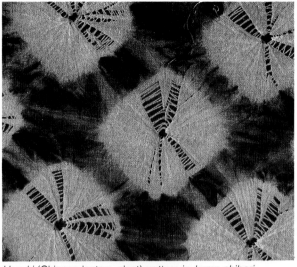

Hozuki (Chinese lantern plant) pattern in *kumo shibori*.

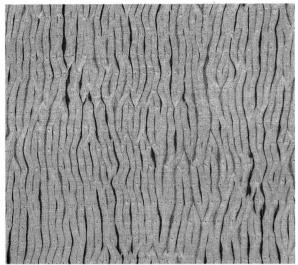

Mokume pattern of sewn tie-dye (*nui shibori*).

Rasen (radiating) tie-dye.

Hinode (sunrise) pattern in sewn tie-dye.

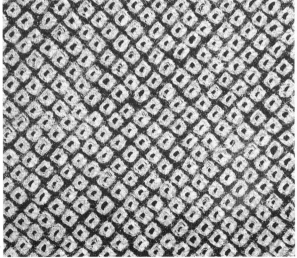

Hitta pattern of fawn-spot tie-dye (*kanoko shibori*).

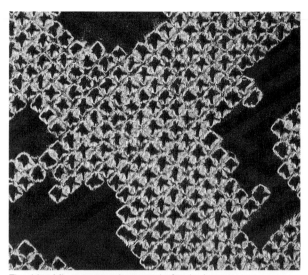

The *hitta* Miura pattern is named after its inventor.

Yukihana (snowflake) pattern of *itajime* (wooden board) tie-dye.

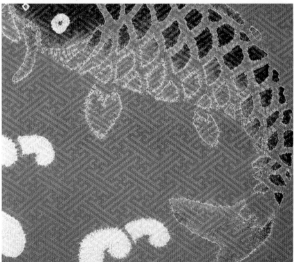

Kawamaki (leather capping) pattern of *makiage shibori*.

Dammono (divided) pattern of *oke shibori*.

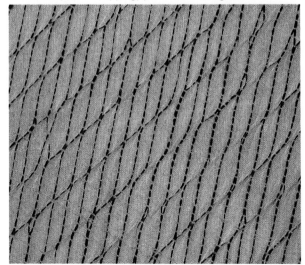

The *amime* (net) pattern of *arashi shibori*.

Yuzen
Multicolored Paste-Resist Dyeing

The Edo period was a time of creativity. Throughout Japan, local governments developed and encouraged the products of regional industry. The capital city of Edo was a hotbed of new ideas. This period was characterized by a flamboyance in dress. Not only were members of the elite samurai class often in debt due to excessive clothing expenses, but the merchants, who gained control of the economy in this period, also began to dress extravagantly. In defiance of the shogunate's sumptuary laws, the common people clamored for new textile designs.

A new dyeing technique called *yuzen* developed around 1700 in response to this

This *yuzen kosode* depicts a falcon perched on a folding screen. Embroidery is effectively used for details such as the falcon's jesses. Edo period. Tokyo National Museum.

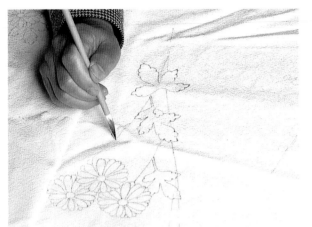
In the *yuzen* process, designs are first drawn with *aobana* liquid.

The *aobana* lines are next covered with paste resist.

After applying the paste resist, dye is painted on with a brush.

demand. This new art form, developed by and named after a fan painter named Miyazaki Yuzensai, was distinguished by its beautiful colors and pictorial designs. Over the years it developed into a major textile art. *Yuzen* was originally produced in the city of Kyoto, where the waters of the Kamo River were ideal for rinsing the bolts of fabric after the dyeing process, and in Kaga Province. From about 1665, with Lord Maeda's patronage, Kaga became a center of art, industry, and learning, on a par with Kyoto. Lord Maeda's love of fine fabrics and the arts was well known, and with his encouragement of weaving and dyeing, Kaga silk and Kaga *yuzen* became famous. Later *yuzen* was also made in Edo and known as Edo *yuzen*.

Yuzen is divided into two basic types, freehand paste drawing *(tegaki) yuzen* and stencil *(kata) yuzen*, according to the method of paste application used. Freehand *yuzen* starts with a small version of the design on paper. It is enlarged to its final size as it is drawn onto the kimono silk with fugitive blue *aobana* liquid (an extract of the spiderwort plant). During most of the steps of the *yuzen* process, the silk is stretched on pliable bamboo rods called *shinshi* to allow the craftsman to draw and brush-dye the fabric.

With the *shinshi* in place, sticky rice-paste resist *(mochiko)* of a fine consistency is drawn on the fabric along the blue *aobana* lines, using a waterproof paper tube with a small metal tip. Then a thin liquid soybean extract *(gojiru)* is spread over the paste and fabric. When dry, the paste works as a resist, keeping the dye

Section of a Kyo *yuzen furisode* in stunning colors, with tie-dye (Kyo fawn spot) and couched gold thread.

inside its borders, while the soybean extract further reduces the chance of unwanted running and aids in the absorption of the dye into the silk. For even spreading of the dyes, water is brushed over the area to be colored and the dye is then applied with a small, flat brush. After steaming the silk to set the dye, the paste is rinsed off, leaving delicate white lines that outline the colorful motifs and pictures of the design.

To protect the completed design during later dyeing, an additional coat of paste is applied over this area and the background dye is brushed on. After a final steaming, the paste is washed out again and the fabric is stretched on *shinshi* to dry. This delicately decorated silk is ready to be hand-stitched into a kimono which will be protected in a paper wrapper (*tatoshi*) until worn.

The other, modern method of *yuzen* dyeing, using stencil resist, is similar except the dye-infused paste is spread over the cloth through a number of stencils. When the paste is rinsed out, the dye remains in the silk.

Various colors of dye-infused paste used in stencil *yuzen*.

51

A Kyo *yuzen* kimono with a banquet scene at a palace depicted in bright hues. The garden in full bloom is surrounded by decorative curtains.

Pretty flower motifs of a *yuzen* stencil.

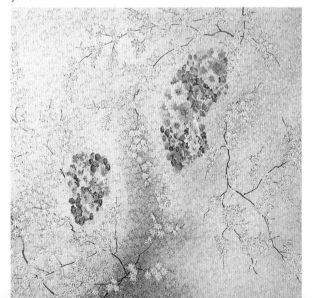

Yuzen is also categorized according to the places in which it is dyed. Each locale gives its own flavor and feeling to its work. Kyo (Kyoto) *yuzen* is aristocratic in design and motifs. Its bright colors contrast with the deeper and more subtly shaded colors of Kaga *yuzen*, dyed in Kaga Province using a special plum-juice dye produced there. Another characteristic of Kaga *yuzen* is the realism of its designs. For example, autumn leaves depicted in Kaga *yuzen* may show even the brownish stains or holes of insect damage. Kaga *yuzen* always

Iris flowers in a variety of hues depicted by the Kaga *yuzen* dyer Uzan Kimura, a Living National Treasure.

Section of a Kaga *yuzen* kimono entitled *Poetry of Flowers*, by Uzan Kimura. The huge bouquet of blossoms is arranged in a Kutani ceramic vase.

stands alone—it is never combined with embroidery, gold or silver imprint, or other embellishment. The Edo *yuzen* of Tokyo is more flamboyant and bolder in color and design, reflecting the world of the theater and objects of daily life, such as vegetables, fish, paper umbrellas, festival dancing, bridges, and drums—motifs influenced by the aesthetic of the Genroku era.

Yuzen is combined with other dyeing and decorative methods to create symbolic motifs appropriate to different seasons, occasions, and the age and social role of the wearer.

Kako Moriguchi, designated a Living National Treasure, is the consummate *yuzen* artist. He incorporates into his dyeing a technique that creates images reminiscent of laquerware strewn with small geometrically shaped pieces of gold leaf. In place of the gold

Gold leaf is also frequently applied to *yuzen* fabrics.

Formal Edo *yuzen furisode* for a young woman with the auspicious symbol of the crane and embroidery. Kuniko Kishimoto collection.

Section of a formal Edo *yuzen* kimono with a Gagaku (music and dance of the ancient court) motif on crepe silk. Akiko Ueshima collection.

leaf, he sprinkles bits of dried paste over damp silk, arranging them carefully. These bits of paste work as a resist against the dye. When he brushes the dye onto the silk, the shapes of the paste remain on the fabric. This technique, called *maki nori*, creates a texture that can be used as background design or incorporated into major motifs according to the desires of the artist.

The moon and plum blossoms are gracefully expressed in *yuzen* obi by Terutaro Arai.

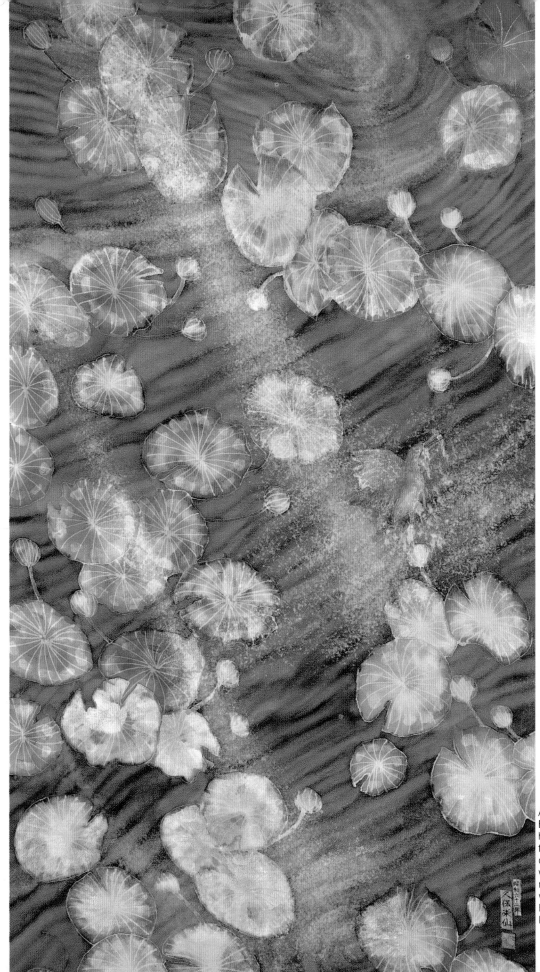

A wall hanging by Eisen Kubo using his original *yuzen* technique to depict rippling water, shimmering reflections of light, water lilies, and a brightly colored kingfisher.

Semiformal kimono entitled *Lingering Snow* by Kako Moriguchi, a Living National Treasure. The bamboo leaves are drawn by the yuzen process and the snow depicted by Moriguchi's *maki nori* gold-flake technique. Crafts Gallery, National Museum of Modern Art.

Katazome
Stencil Dyeing

One of the many traditional dyeing techniques from China is stencil dyeing, or *katazome*, as it is known and still practiced in Japan. Stencils

were first used in the Heian period to decorate leather, and during the Kamakura period a method of stencil dyeing on fabric was in use. By the sixteenth century, this technique had been perfected. The isolation of the Edo period brought *katazome* to full flower, and it

Tanks of permission juice.

Making a stencil of a flower design.

Paper for stencils drying after persimmon juice has been applied to the rice paper.

Extreme care and skill are needed in making a stencil for the highly detailed patterns of *same komon*.

continued as a popular dyeing technique until modern technology and changing tastes in fashion nearly brought it to an end during the Meiji period. For its revival we are indebted to the Mingei, or Folk Crafts, movement and artisans such as Keisuke Serizawa and Toshijiro Inagaki, as well as to the Japanese government's recognition of superior craftsmen and their works.

The word *katazome* is derived from a combination of two Japanese words, *kata*, meaning stencil and *some*, (pronounced in compounds as *zome*), meaning dye. *Katazome* refers to the process of fabric dyeing that employs a water-soluble paste-resist which is applied to the fabric through a cut stencil. The qualities of precision and repetition characteristic of *katazome* are due to the durable stencil paper and a water-soluble rice-paste resist. The stencil paper is made by gluing together several layers of *washi* (paper made from the *kozo*, or paper mulberry plant),

Dyed fabrics drying in the sun.

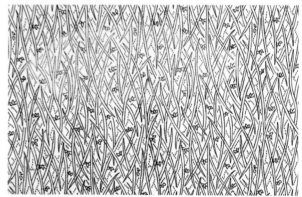

The finished work.

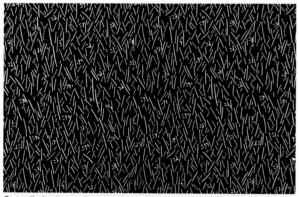

Stencil dyeing using two stencils. The main stencil.

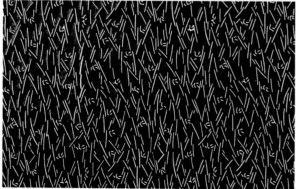

The second stencil.

Inserting silk threads in a stencil to strengthen the most delicate parts.

60

Flowers, rocks, and birds are depicted in vibrant colors and designs by Toshiko Soeda.

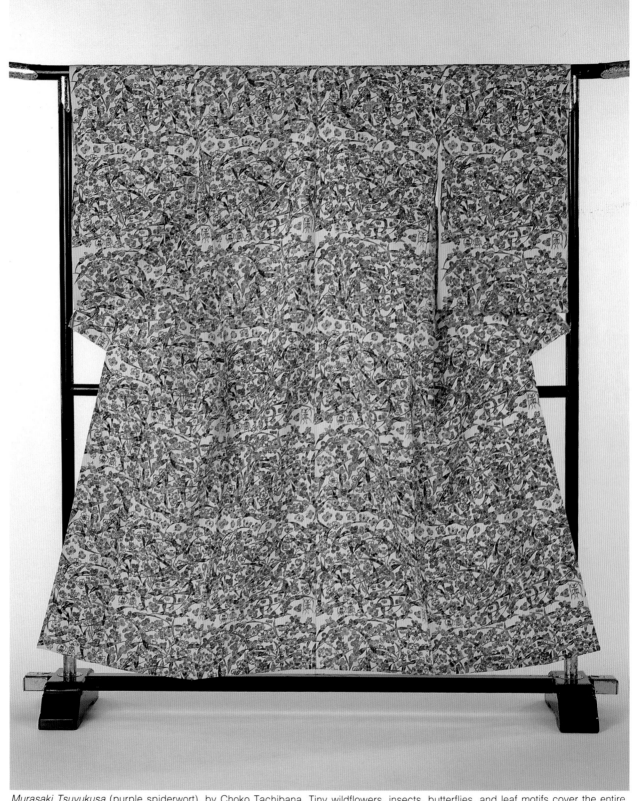

Murasaki Tsuyukusa (purple spiderwort), by Choko Tachibana. Tiny wildflowers, insects, butterflies, and leaf motifs cover the entire surface of the silk crepe.

Kamikochi, a playful depiction of highland scenery by Nobuo Sekiguchi.

treating it with persimmon juice, and smoking it for several days. This extremely durable paper, strengthened by the persimmon tannin and the smoke, can withstand long exposure to moisture and yet can be cut precisely into intricate or bold designs with a very clear edge. Using razor-sharp knives and tools especially created to form unique shapes, precise designs are cut out.

The rice-paste resist, which protects the fabric from the dye, is extremely durable under limited exposure to moisture. At the same time, it can create a very fine design and can be completely washed from the fabric. Made from a mixture of rice flour and rice bran (*nuka*), it is first steamed, then kneaded to the proper consistency for even spreading.

Before the paste is applied, the stencil must be cut. The design is drawn on transparent paper that is then applied directly to the stencil paper with wax. With a very sharp knife both layers are cut. The stencil is then reinforced

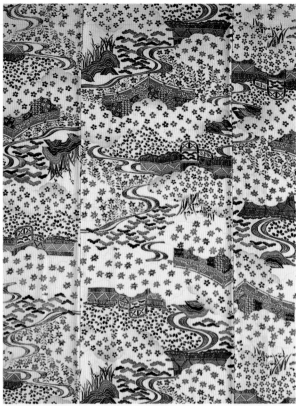

This silk crepe has been stencil dyed with motifs of pine, iris, maple, blue bellflower, flowing water, rustic fences, and festive outdoor curtains. Akiko Ueshima collection.

Stencil-dyed cotton *yukata* fabric of this type is considered appropriate for young women. Seung Kim collection.

These stencil-dyed cotton hand towels are also used as headbands.

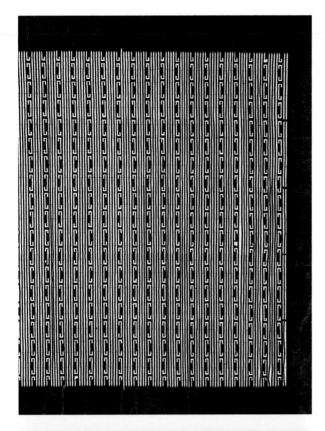

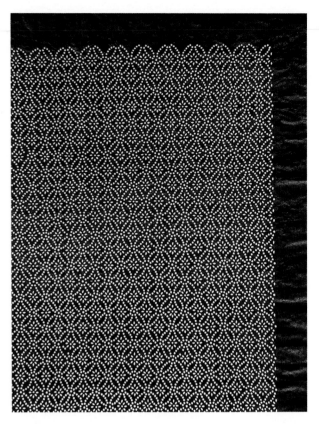

Samples of *komon* stencils.

either with fine silk threads, which are laid between the layers of the stencil, or silk gauze, which is applied to the outside of the paper. The stencil is soaked in water to make it pliable, enabling an accurate fit over the fabric. Then the paste is spread over the stencil with a wooden spatula. This process is repeated as often as necessary to complete the design. When the paste is dry, a sizing of soybean extract liquid is applied to it and the fabric, and then the dye is applied. The dyed fabric is left for several days to cure. Then the paste is removed by soaking it in water, and the design becomes visible. Traditionally, each step was performed by a specific artisan, but some craftsmen today complete the entire process alone.

Katazome textiles were developed as a substitute for more ornate fabrics, to be worn by commoners. Dyers were encouraged to imitate the motifs of sumptuous embroideries, appliques, *shibori*, and silk weaves for use on cotton kimono. With the help of the stencil cutters, they developed many new designs. Stripes, clouds, grasses, flowers, trees, basket weaves, bamboo, and other motifs decorated the new textiles. The stencil cutters from Ise, the stencil center of Japan, sent their designs all over the country to be sold by itinerant salesmen, and they still practice their trade today. Antique stencils can usually be found at the flea markets held regularly throughout Japan.

Komon means small crests and is a pattern of small, all-over repeating motifs. Originally it was mostly used in dyeing leather and bast fibers, and later it was used on silk. *Komon* patterns are created by applying rice-paste resist through a paper stencil and then dyeing the cloth a single color. The sizes of motifs vary, ranging from life-size depictions of blossoms to tiny, pin-point dots. One of the finest *komon* fabrics is called *same* (sharkskin) *komon*, and it was first used for the ceremonial attire of Edo-period samurai, the garment known as *kamishimo*. Early Edo-period *komon* on silk shows a simple geometric arrangement of three to seven dots reserved in white on blue. Soon kimono fabric with various kinds of *komon* designs was widely appreciated by women in Edo for its subdued, elegant coloring and regular arrangement, and *komon* fabrics were used for both informal and semiformal kimonos. The popularity of the fabric in the shogun's capital gave rise to the name Edo *komon*, by which it is often known today.

Samples of *komon* fabrics.

Bingata

Stencil Dyeing of Okinawa

Okinawa, a group of islands south of Kyushu, is separated from the mainland of Japan not only by water but by different cultural influences, climate, and weather patterns. Trade with distant and nearby countries has always been an important part of its economy. For all of these reasons, Okinawan textile art has developed along a unique path.

China, the South Pacific islands, Korea, and Japan have all made their cultural presence felt in the textiles of Okinawa, adding to the available storehouse of colors, motifs, and techniques. In the fourteenth century, trade routes extended from these islands to Sumatra and Ming China, a country that demanded tribute from Okinawa and sent textiles back in return. These cultural exchanges infused the Okinawan Islands with new ideas.

This influence is seen in *bingata* (red stencil), Okinawa's most outstanding dyeing technique. Its characteristic bright colors are a result of the cultural exchange with the South Pacific Islands. Its most distinctive color, vermilion, plus yellow and blue pigments, are applied in their pure form or combined to create complementary colors (such as purple or orange). These are softened by shading (adding a dark color over the original light color), and blurring the edges to accent the design.

In the past, *bingata* with large designs in bright colors made by using several stencils was restricted to the wealthy and the nobility. In addition, it was used in creating dance costumes and courtesans' robes. The color yellow, regarded as equivalent to gold, was worn only by royalty—as was the custom in China. Brown and blue-black were worn by peasants.

Motifs were important. Some, both Japanese and foreign, were used for the

Applying coloring in *bingata*.

Sakuko Komada expresses the image of a garden with colorful flowers.

The banana tree, a typical plant of Okinawa, is used as a motif in clear and refreshing colors.

purpose of protecting the wearer from harm, while others were religious or simply narrative. Dragonflies and butterflies were "souls of departed spirits." Birds, paulownia, bamboo, clouds, phoenixes, bats, and waves were indications of the influence of Ming China, while iris designs, especially when combined with water, were a symbol of Okinawa's links with Japan. Another interesting reminder of Okinawa's exchange with Japan was its use of snow motifs in its designs. Since there is no snow in tropical Okinawa, it is assumed that this motif came from Japan.

Bingata, like most handicrafts, has suffered from the incursion of technology and rising costs of production, but there are craft masters who have helped revive this particular area of textile art. Perhaps the most famous of the recent artisans in this field and the most influential in its revival was Keisuke Serizawa, who was a Living National Treasure. His beautiful *bingata* designs are both functional and decorative, and his kimono are among the most outstanding.

Today's pigments are slightly different from the imported pigments used in the past, but the dyes still show the bright, colorful influences of the contacts the Okinawans made with the South Sea Islanders and the Chinese.

A close-up view of a lively design of traditional Okinawan motifs—flowers and water—in bright colors against a yellow background.

A pretty landscape in bright red on a light blue background, by Sakuko Komada.

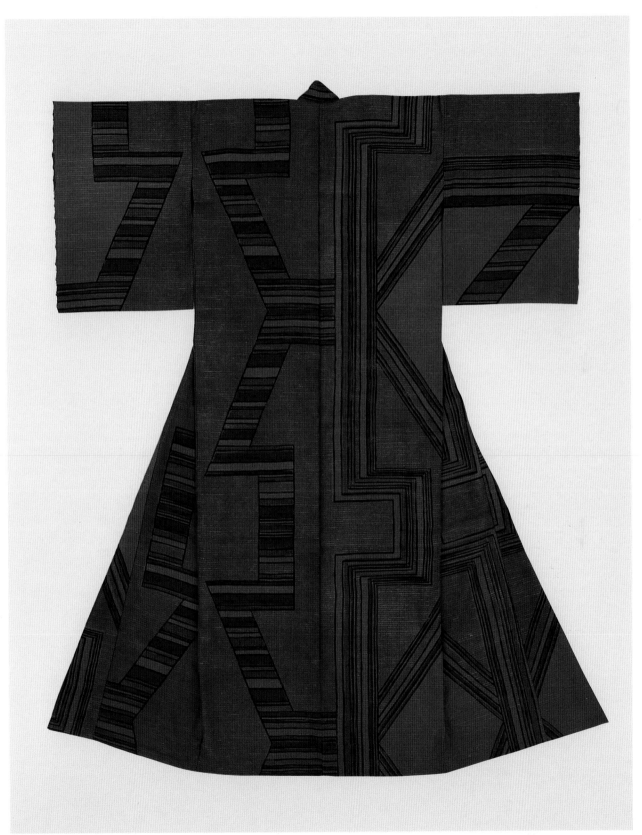

Indigo and vegetable dyes are used by Sakuko Komada to create the abstract design of this blue and green kimono.

Autumn in Kamakura, by Keisuke Serizawa, a Living National Treasure, is handsomely rendered in subtle colors.

Tsutsugaki
Freehand Paste-Resist Dyeing

This freely drawn design technique has a spontaneity not found in most other textile design. Its bold, unique motifs, outlined in white, contrast with its deep indigo blue, and its bright colors are beautifully rendered on cotton. Unlike the repeated designs of stencil dyeing, large, freehand motifs dominate the overall design of *tsutsugaki* textiles. Commoners have used *tsutsugaki* to decorate clothing, *furoshiki*, bedding, banners, and even children's towels since the Edo period. It was customary then for a bride to be given a trousseau by her family when she married, consisting of all the clothing and household textile items she would need during her married life. As the commoners did not have access to expensive silks, these resourceful people used cotton to create beautifully designed utilitarian items. With indigo dye and paste resist, they had their family crests and symbols of good luck, such as the phoenix, lion, crane, turtle, pine trees, and paulownia, dyed onto the trousseau items. The specialists who created these masterpieces worked long and hard to attain textiles of strength, beauty, and durability.

Rice paste is once again the resist used to draw the white lines that delineate these vibrant designs. With a waterproof paper cone (called a *tsutsu*), the paste is drawn onto the fabric, following lines previously laid out with *aobana*. After a coating of liquid soybean extract has been brushed over the material, pigments are applied to the designs. These colored areas are then covered with paste and sprinkled with sawdust to protect them should they come in

A *tsutsugaki* wrapping cloth with auspicious motifs of pine, plum, and tortoise, with a family crest.

A bridal wrapping cloth to wrap and carry the new bedding that is part of her wedding-day trousseau. The patchwork bag with the string is a rice bag.

73

Sash to carry a baby on the back. The family crest can be seen on the fabric.

Applying paste resist with a waterproof paper cone (*tsutsu*) along a line traced in *aobana*.

contact with other pasted areas in the dye vat. Then the fabric is put into the indigo vat.

When indigo-dyed fabric first comes out of the vat, it is a light green, but contact with the air causes the dye to oxidize, and its color changes to deep blue. Additional dips in the dye vat are carried out until the desired depth of color is reached. After this dyeing process is finished, the fabric is soaked in water to remove the paste, and the piece is stretched on bamboo *shinshi* rods to dry. Where the paste lines were, white lines remain, outlining the pictures painted by the artist.

A *happi* coat with a rabbit motif by the Konjin Workshop.

The *tsutsugaki* technique was born from the use of three plants: cotton, brought from Korea in the fifteenth century; rice, Japan's staple food; and indigo, which was grown throughout the country. *Tsutsugaki* flourished over the two hundred sixty years of the Edo period. Fortunately, the recent movement to revive the Japanese folk crafts is helping a number of artist-craftsmen to continue to create *tsutsugaki* textiles according to traditional techniques.

A *tsutsugaki* shop curtain (*noren*) by the Konjin Kobo Tsutsugaki Workshop.

A wrapping cloth decorated with a Chinese lion and peony (*karajishi botan*) motif by the Konjin Workshop.

4

Woven Textiles

Nishijin ori textile

Noh play, *Izutsu*, by Tetsunojo Kanze.

An empty battle encampment may seem a strange birthplace for the exquisite shimmering silks of obi and Noh costumes. Yet it was the West Camp, or Nishijin, which became the weaving center of Japan from the late fifteenth century. For more than a decade, terrible civil wars had engulfed Kyoto, and the weavers had fled the city. When they returned, they gathered in what had been the camp of the western division defending the capital, and many of them are still there today. In Nishijin the weavers produced exquisite brocades, gauzes, and twills, using looms that employed "draw boys" who sat atop the machines and pulled the "flowers" (the colored warp threads) according to the patterns called out by the master. Reminiscent of the practice of pattern calling in the carpet workshops of Asia, this technique disappeared when manually operated Jacquard looms, programmed by a series of punched cards, replaced the old draw looms in the nineteenth century. Weaving masters still use the Jacquard loom to lace their silk filaments into *kara ori* (float-weave brocade) and *nishiki*.

Hand weaving has been a mainstay in the human library of creative and practical processes since prehistoric times. As early as the Yayoi period (200 B.C.–A.D. 250), Japan had woven fabrics. Bast fibers were woven on backstrap looms, simple weaving devices attached at one end to the weaver and at the other end to a stationary object such as a tree. By the Nara period (552–794), woven goods were produced by advanced techniques such as *nishiki* and *ra* (complex gauze weave). Over the centuries, the fortunes of the weaving industry have vacillated, but Nishijin has remained the center of Japanese textile art since the days of Toyotomi Hideyoshi.

While dyers embellish a piece of fabric that has already been made, weavers create their designs as they weave, making the design an integral part of the material. These woven motifs can consist of contrasting colored threads woven together in patterns, or threads of the same color woven in a way that light will show their patterns. Woven design, by its nature, has technical limitations, but they are marvelously overcome by the great agility and creativity of master weavers.

The basic process of weaving involves the intertwining at right angles of two yarns to create a flat piece of fabric. This is accomplished by attaching a warp to a loom of some description and weaving the weft threads until a desired length of fabric has been produced.

The three basic weaves used in Japan are: *hira ori* (plain or flat weave), *aya ori* (twill weave), and *shusu ori* (satin float weave), each of which has numerous variations.

An old woman absorbed in weaving *tsumugi* fabric.

A *kara ori* Noh costume with woven motifs of bamboo blinds and maple leaves. Edo period. Eisei Bunko Collection.

Hira Ori

Plan or Flat Weave

The simplest weave, and probably the oldest, *hira ori* is produced by weaving one warp thread over one weft thread and then under the next, resulting in an even, flat weave with no woven patterning. This kind of fabric can be dense or open, depending on the spacing of the threads. *Kasuri*, Saga *nishiki* (gold brocade), *tsumugi*, and *tsuzure ori* (tapestry weave) are examples of *hira ori*. *Karami ori* (silk gauze) and striped and checked fabrics are important variations of this weave.

Kasuri: Dyed and Woven Textiles

This unique fabric traveled from India to Indonesia (where it is called *ikat*) and the South Pacific. Then, by way of Okinawa or China, it came to Japan, where it developed into a popular folk craft. Distinguished by its irregular geometric designs, *kasuri* is created by weaving together yarn that has been predyed with a pattern. This yarn is resist dyed by binding it with string in predetermined areas dictated by the desired design, then immersing it in the dye. When these bindings are removed, the white "splashed" design areas are revealed, and the yarn is ready to be woven into fabric.

Three types of design are possible with this plain weave. The fairly vertical, geometric designs of *tategasuri* (*kasuri* becomes *gasuri* in many compounds) are formed when the vertical warp threads are design dyed and woven with monochromatic, horizontal weft threads. *Yokogasuri* uses pattern-dyed weft threads to create free-form picture images. One highly specialized form of this type of weaving, *egasuri*, or "picture *kasuri*," is the weaving of cranes, tortoises, flowers, clouds, dog footprints, and other designs into indigo-dyed fabric. The third major type of *kasuri*,

Tying the threads for resist before dyeing.

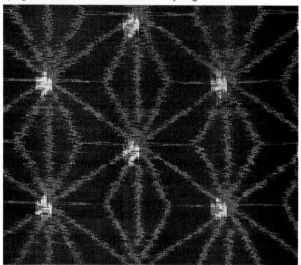
Yokogasuri.

Yokogasuri.

80

Different patterns and shades of indigo blue in Kurume *gasuri*.

Tateyokogasuri.

The Ryukyu *gasuri* of Okinawa.

Tateyokogasuri.

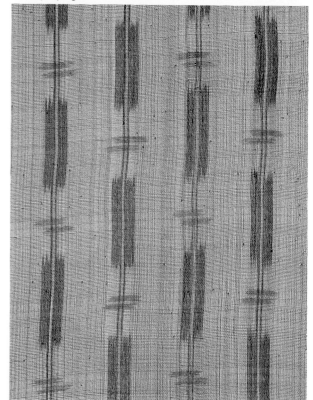

Typical *bashofu* fabric.

tateyokogasuri, uses both warp and weft threads that have been design resist-dyed. This weaving is identifiable by the completely white areas of its geometric designs. The charm of *kasuri* lies in the simplicity of the designs and the fuzziness of their edges, caused by slight irregularities in the dyeing of the individual threads.

In the *kasuri* of Okinawa, large, abstract, geometric motifs were reserved for royalty and the upper classes, while smaller ones were for the lower classes. Color combinations such as pink with dark blue designs indicated the upper class, and yellow combined with red, green, or violet were only for royalty.

Cotton was introduced to the islands of Okinawa about 1622, followed shortly by silk (both of which augmented the preexisting bast fibers), which was considered precious. Until that time, ramie and *bashofu*, a unique fabric made from boiling, scraping, and splitting the fibers of the *ito basho*, a type of banana tree, had been the time-honored textiles worn by the Okinawans and often decorated by *kasuri* techniques.

Kasuri motifs range from several inches in width and height to only a fraction of an inch.

The smallest, *jofu*, distinguished by minute hatchmarks, was worn by men as late as the middle of the present Showa era. These casual kimono made from ramie are still worn. The names like "cat's paw" and "mosquito *kasuri*" give apt description of some of their motif shapes.

From the Edo period, the lower classes used cotton or hemp *kasuri* clothing, bed coverings, and other utilitarian textiles. In place of the more luxurious silk weaves, they used *tsumugi* (pongee), a less costly silk spun from textured floss, which was derived from leftover silk cocoons. Its matte finish gave it the appearance of cotton, thus providing the perfect answer for those who wished to wear silk but were not allowed to do so by law. The favored motifs for this fine fabric, which required a year's work for the weaving of one kimono, were *kasuri* and stripes. *Tsumugi* is still woven in several places today. Yuki *tsumugi*, from the town of Yuki in Ibaraki Prefecture, and Oshima *tsumugi*, from Amami Oshima Island in Kagoshima Prefecture, are well known, and they have become very expensive fabrics today.

Smoothing the banana-leaf fibers before spinning.

Twisting thread for *tsumugi* while spinning.

Dyed threads drying under the sun.

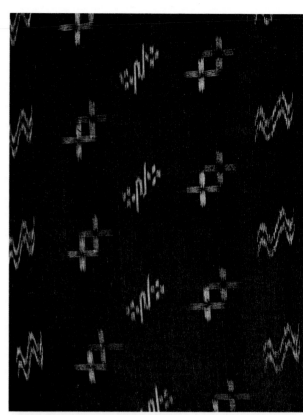

Kumejima *tsumugi* of Kume Island.

The Echigo *jofu* of Niigata Prefecture.

The Miyako *jofu* of Okinawa.

Benibana (safflower) *tsumugi* of Yamagata Prefecture.

Beautiful fragments
of Shinshu *tsumugi*
from Nagano
Prefecture.

Ai Oshima *tsumugi*.

White Oshima *tsumugi*.

Yuki *tsumugi.*

Saga *Nishiki*

An interesting variation of the plain weave was developed in 1820. The wife of a feudal lord, Lord Nabeshima of Saga, needing something to fill her empty hours, devised a complete weaving process which she called Saga *nishiki*.

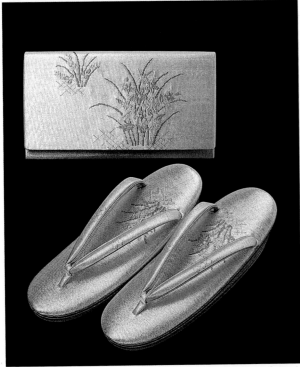

Dressy Saga *nishiki* handbag and *zori* (Japanese formal sandals).

It combined fine, colored silk weft with a gold or silver warp. The shimmering small handbags and accessories seen in the kimono sections of better department stores today are an example of this weaving technique.

Tsuzure Ori

Tapestry, the first purely decorative weaving, has existed in Egypt from as early as 1483 B.C. There is evidence of tapestry weaving in Song-Dynasty China (420–79), and it was a widespread technique during the Tang Dynasty (618–907). This plain weave has been practiced throughout the world, and there are many outstanding examples of this technique: European tapestries, famous for their composition and beauty; *kilim*, the flat weave rugs of Asia; and the Navajo rugs of north America. Chinese tapestry weaving came to

Tsuzure-weave obi in different colors by Keiichi Hoshino.

Tsuzure ori obi woven in bright colors of peonies, cherry blossoms, wisteria, chrysanthemums, and camellias on a flower cart, a symbol of good luck.

89

Japan, where it was called *tsuzure ori*, or fingernail tapestry weave. This fine silk weave was assimilated into the Japanese weaving repertory and became established as a domestic product by the year 1400.

Tapestry weavers employ a number of shuttles for the weft, each one passing a certain thread back and forth over only the area needed for the design and surface, instead of using a single weft thread passing through the entire width of the warp from selvage to selvage. In that way, one row of woven material can consist of several colors, and free-form designs in various shapes can be created.

The *tsuzure ori* weaver's fingernails are basic tools, used along with a wooden comb to beat down the weft of the tapestry. The weaver files three nails on each hand into a serrated edge and uses one nail until it has been worn down, then moves on to the next nail, reserving the other nails until they have

Artisan weaving *tsuzure ori*.

grown back.

The sumptuous fabric woven in this way is seen today in stage curtains, temple hangings, festival cart decorations, and obi. Some small shops in Nishijin turn out this beautiful fabric woven by hand, just as it has been done for centuries.

Karami Ori

The elegant silk gossamers *ra*, *sha*, and *ro*, whether plain, patterned, or shot through with gold, are members of the gauze family and are all known in Japan as *karami ori*, a loose open mesh.

The simplest weave, *sha*, is followed in complexity by *ra*, the warp threads of which create intricate designs by running at diagonal angles to the weft. *Ro* is distinguished by strips of densely woven material separated by an open weave.

Floating over the stage of the Noh theater, glistening over the robes of Buddhist monks, or worn as kimono, these transparent silks come to us from ancient history. Gauze originated in Palestine and spread to the West and East, arriving in China as early as 200 B.C. From there it moved on to Japan some time in the seventh century A.D., where by the eighth century, it was produced domestically to be used in Buddhist religious ceremonies and imperial coronations. Examples of eighth-century *ra* and *sha* in the Shosoin collection exhibit these complex weaves used as the base fabric for resist dyeing and embroidered designs.

The secret of these open weave fabrics is the twisting of their fine warp threads in pairs. The weft threads are inserted between the twists, forming an open weave that is strong, beautiful, and cool. Motifs of rippling water and summer flowers are sometimes embroidered on the fabric to give an even cooler feeling in the hot summers.

Flower motifs dyed with the *Kokechi* technique on *ra* fabric. Nara period. Tokyo National Museum.

Unlined summer kimono of purple *ro* fabric with autumn flowers, grasses, insects, and rippling water embroidered in dazzling colors. Edo period. Tokyo National Museum.

Light gray *ro*-fabric visiting kimono (*homongi*) with plovers at the seashore stencil-dyed in cool colors.

Nagaginu Noh costume mainly used for female dancers. Outer jacket of *ro* fabric woven elegantly in chrysanthemum, pampas grass, and dew motifs with gold and silver and color threads. Edo period. Eisei Bunko collection.

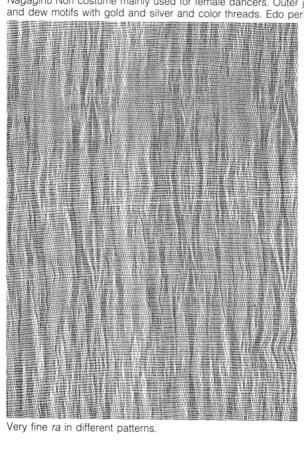

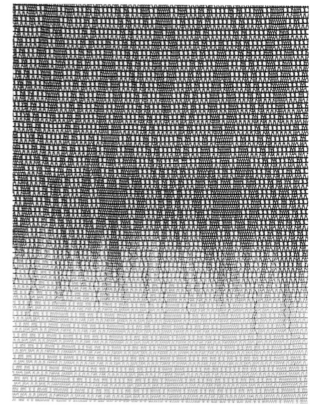

Very fine *ra* in different patterns.

Pretty *sha* in different motifs.

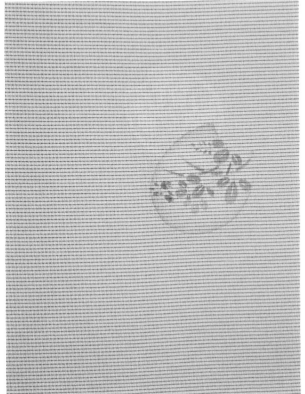

Delicately stencil-dyed weft *ro* fabric.

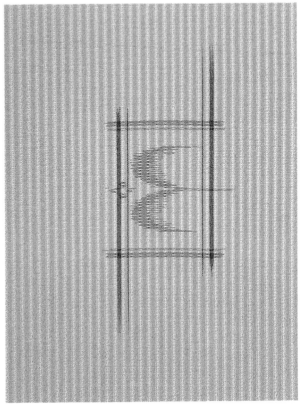

Woven with dyed threads. Warp *ro* fabric.

Shima and *Koshi:* Stripes and Checks

These extremely fashionable designs of the Edo period were originally considered rustic and common, possibly because of their simplicity. In the Muromachi period, however, the tea master Kobori Enshu chose these simple patterns for use in the tea ceremony. Their adoption by the Noh and, particularly, Kyogen theaters for use as costumes also added to their prestige. From then on, stripes and checks gradually became popular with the samurai class, who came to wear them for formal occasions. They reached the height of their popularity in the Edo period.

The first stripes were horizontal, created by inserting wefts of colors different from the background. The next step, alternating the warp colors to make vertical stripes, was then quickly followed by combining the two techniques, creating check or plaid designs.

The ease with which stripes and plaids can be woven contributes to the wide variety of designs that can be created in this flat weave. Using only straight lines and different colors of thread, the weaver can make wide or thin stripes, plaids, and squares of any size. Striped fabric came from Europe to China, and it was on Chinese ships that stripes made their way through the islands of Okinawa to the mainland of Japan. *Kanto* stripes—named after the Japanese pronunciation of Canton, the area of China from which these imported silks came to Japan—soon found a home among the commoners.

Bright *Kanto* stripes. Sixteenth-seventeenth century. Tokyo National Museum.

Plaid *tamba* cloth from Sasayama in Hyogo Prefecture is woven from nubby silk weft and cotton warp, and is popular for bedding. *Ki hachijo* (yellow *hachijo*) from Hachijo Island is a high-quality silk plaid that was popular during the Edo period and is still woven there. Using natural dyes such as pampas grass *(kariyasu)* to achieve its characteristic yellow, the *madami* plant for brown, and the natural iron oxides in the mud of the island, the dyers produce rich colors. In Akita Prefecture, a similar but less complex fabric called Akita *hachijo* is dyed and woven by famers' wives in imitation of *ki hachijo*.

Okinawan stripes are usually of the warp variety. Simple rod stripes of varying colors are also popular, along with plaid weaves and the checkerboard *(goban)* pattern. Not technically the same but also geometric in design are the raised patterns *(hana ori)* which are produced when extra threads are added to the woven fabric.

The Ueda *tsumugi* of Nagano Prefecture.

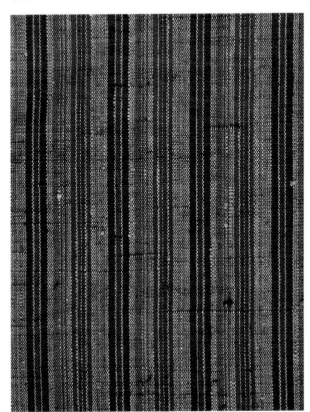

The Nambu *tsumugi* of Iwate Prefecture.

The Shinshu *tsumugi* of Nagano Prefecture.

Striped silk crepe *kosode* embellished with embroidery. Edo period. Tokyo National Museum.

Benibana tsumugi from Yamagata Prefecture.

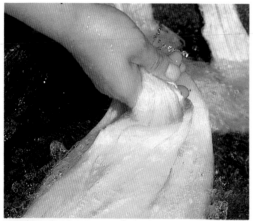

Kariyasu (pampas grass)-dyed threads to weave *kihachijo*.

Mud dyeing to obtain a brown color for *tsumugi* on Oshima Island.

Kihachijo.

Benibana tsumugi from Yamagata Prefecture.

Oitama *tsumugi* from Yamagata Prefecture.

Aya Ori

Twill Weave

Aya ori basically relies on the reflected light to reveal its patterns, which are woven by passing a weft thread over or under two or more warp threads. The designs vary with the direction of the pattern weave. The pattern can be woven on a plain or twill background, or it can be reversed with a twilled pattern on a twilled background going in the same or opposite direction as that of the pattern.

When Emperor Shomu died in 756, his grieving widow, Empress Dowager Komyo, donated all his personal belongings to the Todaiji temple at Nara. Among these items was an extensive number of eighth-century textiles, which have been preserved there over the years in the Shosoin Repository. When considered with the seventh-century Horyuji textile collection, now in the Tokyo National Museum, we have a comparatively thorough knowledge of the textiles of the Nara period.

During that time, Japan enjoyed extensive trade with Tang China, and assimilated many ideas from this neighbor. Among these was the layout of Nara, the capital of Japan at the time, which was patterned after a Chinese city, and the encouragement of Buddhism, which resulted in the construction of many temples and the importation of continental technology. Also important was the influence felt among the textile workers, who assimilated Tang motifs into their designs and learned to weave in the same way the imported cloth was made.

The Shosoin and Horyuji collections contain examples of both the imported and domestically woven fabrics (among which are *nishiki, ayaori, ra,* and *sha*) as well as dyed works, represented by the three resist dyeing methods described earlier (bound resist, wax resist, and carved wooden block resist). *Aya* was woven in Japan for the first time in the second or third century, and had spread to many parts of the country by the eighth century. *Aya ori* is a soft, shiny fabric characterized by its diagonally woven patterns. Important varieties of the *aya* weave are *nishiki* and *kara ori*.

Nishiki

A multicolored patterned weave, *nishiki* first came to Japan from China when the King of Wei made a gift of it to Empress Jingu in the form of bolts of silk woven with a multicolored dragon motif. Japan had received gifts of silkworm eggs in A.D. 188 from China and in the year 200 had received woven silk from Korea. After Empress Jingu lead invasion forces into Korea in the early third century, she returned to Japan with a Korean weaver who produced the first domestically woven patterned silks in Japan. These monochromatic fabrics, an early form of *aya*, were geometric in design on a plain-weave ground. Japanese nobility, captivated by these exotic fabrics, prompted the establishment of a domestic silk industry, and within one hundred years mulberry trees had been planted throughout Japan. In the year 645, special looms were constructed for the purpose of weaving

An artisan weaving *nishiki*.

intricate *nishiki*. By the sixteenth century, both imported and domestic *nishiki* were very popular and had become an important Japanese product. In the stability and opulence of the Momoyama period, *nishiki* production progressed, and by the Edo period it was at its most advanced level.

Nishiki means "beautiful color combination." It refers particularly to patterned silks woven with an uneven number of several colors, usually blue, red, yellow, reddish purple, and green.

Nishiki is a flat brocade-like weave, sometimes twilled, distinguished by the fact that the weft threads go from selvage to selvage, unbroken. Warp *nishiki* is woven by manipulating a warp of different threads with a weft of a single color for each row. The chromatic combinations of this less complex type are limited by the width of the cloth, which allows only a limited number of warp thread colors. Weft *nishiki* relies on the weaving of weft threads of different colors into a monochromatic warp and is limited only by the number of weft colors available to the weaver.

Hunting scenes, stripes, and the most characteristic *nishiki* motif, flowers, delicately graced sumptuous silks in the Nara period. *Nishiki* played an important role in the elaborate costume of the period. Today *nishiki* is hand woven in Nishijin.

A fragment of old *nishiki* with a Chinese flower motif. Tokyo National Museum.

A *nishiki* obi with a dainty design of flowers and birds, copied from an ancient fabric in the Shosoin collection.

A nishiki obi with a chrysanthemum design.

Kara Ori

As we have seen, at various times in the history of Japanese clothing, the glittering beauty of *nishiki* and the complexity of *tsujigahana* seduced many people into spending vast fortunes on their wardrobes. The shoguns, fearing the effect of this extravagance on the national economy, regularly enacted laws forbidding expensive textiles. *Nishiki*, all-over fawn-spot tie-dye, elaborate embroidery, and various silks were all at some time forbidden by law. Fortunately, these laws often unwittingly encouraged new forms of textile decoration, for as one textile was prohibited, a new one would often spring up to replace it.

Kariginu Noh costume. This is an outer jacket originally worn by a nobleman as a hunting cloak. The front and back hang loosely. Hemp-leaf and scrolling plant design on brocade. Edo period. Eisei Bunko Collection.

Atsuita Noh costume. This is an outer robe worn by male characters. It has contrasting colors and repeated geometric patterns of phoenixes, paulownia, and hail in float-weave brocade. Edo period. Eisei Bunko collection.

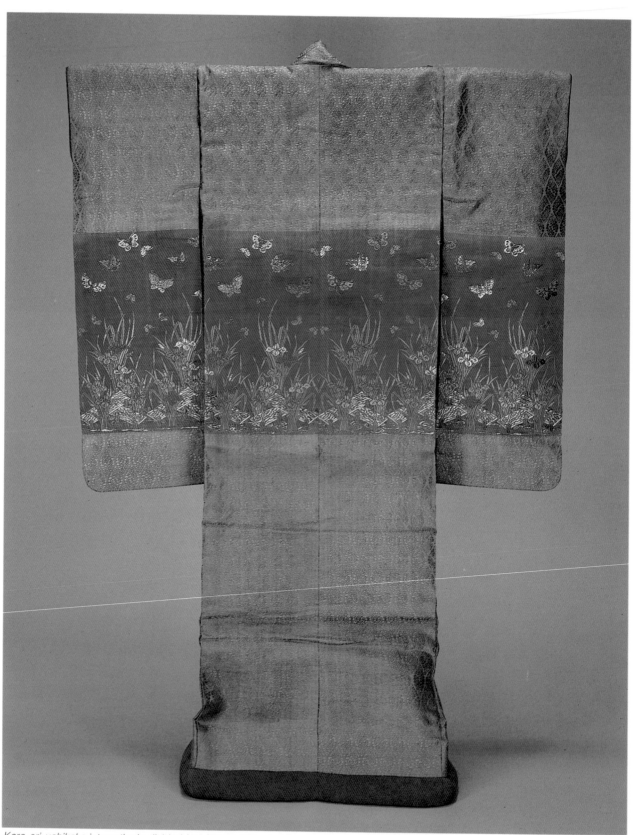

Kara ori uchikake interestingly divided into bands of contrasting colors with a delicate design of butterflies, irises, and eight-arched bridges woven in the middle section. Edo period. Tokyo National Museum.

A *kara ori* Noh costume worn mainly by female characters. Sumptuous in its color combinations and design of flowers and butterflies in float-weave brocade. Edo period. Eisei Bunko collection.

Kara ori obi in stunning colors and designs by Kichitaro Nakajima.

Beautiful *kara ori* outer robe worn by the courtesan Agemaki in a scene from the famous Kabuki play *Sukeroku*.

Flowers, grapes, and bamboo depicted in *kara ori* weave.

Japan of the Momoyama period was strongly influenced by the culture of Ming China, whose rich, gold-decorated silk fabrics were being imported and worn by the nobility. The proliferation of festivals and theatrical and dance performances created a strong demand for these fabrics, prompting Japanese weavers to produce domestic versions for use by both the actors and the audiences. More and more elaborate clothing was required. In this fanciful atmosphere, the technical skills of the weavers were stretched to their limit.

The fabric dubbed *kara ori* ("Chinese weave," but generally known as float-weave brocade) was this native Japanese replacement for the imported Chinese brocades and embroideries. This new type of satin weave employed colored floating threads, which lay on top of the fabric much like embroidery. Later, gold or silver thread was also woven into the material. For the purpose of weaving these rainbow colors into the fabric, the threads were wound on small bobbins. Attached at both ends of the motif, these silk threads floated across the design like embroidered images.

Originally, *kara ori* was the general term used to describe Chinese imported fabrics. Today, in the Noh theater it specifies a stiff costume worn for women's roles, made from Japanese *kara ori* silk, as Chinese silk has not been used since the Momoyama period.

When Noh was first staged, a gift of clothing from a noble was considered a reward for an actor's excellence. The original Noh costumes were probably gifts from the wife of a shogun who wore Chinese *kara ori* robes to the performances and wished to reward an actor for a moving portrayal.

These gifts, kept and treasured by the actor, were then worn in later performances. As the Noh theater acquired the patronage of the mighty and the powerful and became more affluent, *kara ori* costumes were made especially for Noh, incorporating motifs that reflected the character played by the actor wearing the costume.

Today, traditional Noh costumes dazzle us in the theater, while ornate obi and *uchikake* remain in the everyday world to remind us of their traditional roles. The *uchikake*, the most elaborate of the ceremonial robes worn outside the theater, is still worn in the traditional wedding ceremony, over a white kimono.

Shusu Ori

Satin Float Weave

Luxurious fabrics are woven by the satin weave. Each weft thread floats over many warp threads, creating a smooth, shiny surface. *Shusu ori* is even shiner than *nishiki* and dazzles with its lavish patterns in stunning colors, rivaling embroidery in its decorativeness.

Donsu

Donsu, a patterned weave, is a type of damask that relies on the contrast of the pattern directions to reveal its designs, although the design is sometimes intensified by using contrasting colors in the warp and weft. Originally imported from China, *donsu* became a favorite in Japan for tea-ceremony textiles and the mounting of the scroll or wall hangings called *kakemono*. Some favorite *donsu* motifs are squared spirals, checkerboard squares, carp, clouds, and plum blossoms.

Fragment of *donsu*. Fourteenth to fifteenth century. Tokyo National Museum.

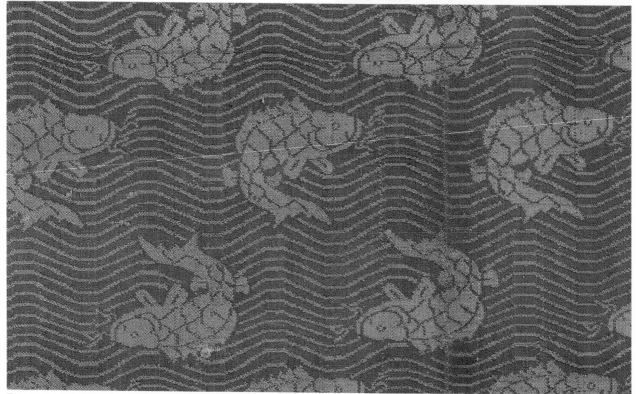

Fragment of *donsu*. Fourteenth to fifteenth century. Tokyo National Museum.

Donsu uchikake embellished with mandarin ducks and iris in a rippling stream. A plum tree in blossom is depicted at the bottom. Edo period. National Museum of Japanese History.

Kinran

This is a small, simple gold design against a background of one plain color. It was brought to Japan from Ming China during the Kamakura period. The fabric patterns of *kinran* are made by inserting thin strips of gold-covered paper thread into the warp on every other row. This twill-weave silk boasts plain-weave gold motifs such as *karakusa*, peony scrolls, chrysanthemums, clematis, dragons, and paulownia. The swatch books of precious fabrics *(meibutsu gire cho)* preserved by temples contain examples of Chinese *kinran*.

A *kinran* tea-container cover. Momoyama period. Tokyo National Museum.

A book covered with shimmering *donsu* fabric.

A *kinran* obi with a peony and scrolling plant design.

5
Needlework and Applied Decoration

Embroidery is an ancient method of decoration that was introduced to Japan in the sixth century. A Chinese embroiderer was brought to Japan by Kibi no Makabi, a Buddhist priest, on his return from China. That Chinese craftsman became the first *nuimonoshi*—a person who embroiders textiles in many-colored threads. At the beginning, embroidery was used to apply additional decoration to woven and dyed cloth, but later embroidered design was used as an alternative for achieving the same effect as brocade, and was considered very valuable.

Quilting on cotton has also been practiced in Japan for utilitarian purposes. Layers of fabric were stitched together in various beautiful and innovative designs to create clothing of warmth and durability.

Shishu
Embroidery

The oldest embroidered piece in Japan, the *Tenjukoku Mandala* (Heavenly Paradise Mandala), in Chuguji temple at Nara, is a piece of silk *ra* executed during the first part of the seventh century. Only a small piece of the original embroidered silk remains intact. It is in the form of Chinese characters stitched in parallel lines of twisted silk thread on the backs of two tortoises. This National Treasure gives us a glimpse into the long history of this art of embroidery in Japan. As early as the Jomon Period, people used fishbone needles for simple stitchery. By the seventh century, creative stitching decorated ceremonial robes for the emperor and the nobility. However, most of the early embroideries were used for Buddhist banners, sewn by friends and relatives of the decreased for the purpose of helping him along his way in heaven.

During the Muromachi Period, embroidery was used as a substitute for expensive brocades. This versatile form of fabric decoration appeared on *kosode* and Noh costumes, which glittered with *nuihaku* (the combination of embroidery and imprinted gold or silver leaf). The softer silks of the Momoyama period were embellished with stitchery, using untwisted silk and gold or silver thread to create small, simple designs. By the end of this affluent era, embroidery had reached its height. Under the patronage of Toyotomi Hideyoshi, fabulous Noh costumes and kimono entirely covered with embroidered designs were created.

In the isolation of the Edo period, embroidered motifs became more Japanese in style and the popularity of this decoration increased. Embroidery was in such high demand that one shogun ordered thirty-two elaborately embroidered kimono over a period of sixteen years. The popularity of this

Embroidered Shakyamuni preaching to the disciples surrounding him. Tang Dynasty, China. National Treasure. Tokyo National Museum.

Gorgeous embroidery work on a black *rinzu kosode* with motifs of pine, bamboo, chrysanthemums, rippling water, snowy herons and baskets in rich colors. Family crest is done by gold couching. Edo period. Tokyo National Museum.

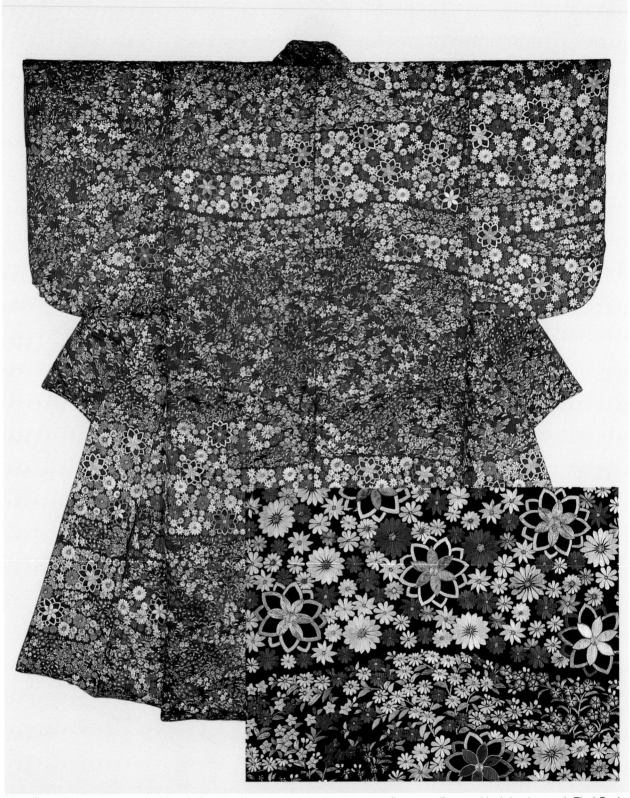

Magnificent Noh costume embroidered all over with exceptionally dainty autumn-flower motifs on a black background. Eisei Bunko collection.

With a thinner thread careful couching is done over the silver or gold thread.

Roundels of plum, chrysanthemum, pine, maple, peony, bamboo, and bellflower in a basket pattern by Mitsuko Kashimura.

Flying birds, weeping cherry tree in bloom, and ocean wave on an obi by Shizuka Kusano.

decorative form soon declined, however, because of its extravagance, and the simpler and less expensive method of applique emerged.

Japanese embroidery employs several stitches, some of which are: French knot *(sagaranui),* dating from the Nara period; the outline satin stitch *(nuikiri);* back-stitch outline *(matsuinui);* satin stitch *(warinui);* and long

Embroidered firewoman's headgear with gold thread couching. Edo period. Tokyo National Museum.

Lower part of kimono embroidered in motifs of pretty flowers, grass, and *shippo tsunagi* (interlocking rings) in bright colors by Shizuka Kusano.

couched stitches *(watashinui).* The gold or silver thread used for couching is made by wrapping silk thread with gold- or silver-covered paper. This thread is applied to the fabric by stitching it down with a very thin filament. Couching is used to highlight dyed kimono and to apply the family crest *(kamon)* used on outer garments for family identification.

Four obi embroidered with different techniques by Hyakutei Hashio. The flowers almost seem to be dyed.

A woman's hanten (short work jacket) with various patterns by Eiko Yoshida.

Sashiko and Kogin
Quilting

In contrast to the delicate, ornamental silk embroideries, *sashiko* (quilting on cotton) stands out for its creative sturdiness and utilitarianism. Originating in the northern part of Honshu Island, *sashiko* was used to prolong the life of the indigo-dyed work clothes worn by farmers, fishermen, and their families. Both the men and the women of these families worked at this craft. Once they obtained cotton fabrics, they dyed them with indigo, which strengthens the cotton. Using heavy white thread, they made rows of long stitches through several layers of cotton or ramie fabric. The stitches took the shape of familiar geometric motifs, such as the hemp leaf and the tortoise shell. The result was an artistic garment that was delightful to see and warm as well, for the added layers of fabric made an insulated garment.

When these layered fabrics were stitched closely together with straight, parallel rows of stitches, an extremely durable fabric resulted. Firemen soon saw the value of this fabric and used it for the protective coats they wore when fighting fires. The firemen's coats were not only functinal but very beautiful, for while the outsides were decorated only with a simple motif, the insides were often beautifully hand painted.

Over the years, *sashiko*'s function has became basically ornamental. New curvilinear motifs have been adopted and the traditional indigo fabrics have been supplemented with other types of textiles. utilitarian items such as clothing, placements, and pot holders are, however, still made.

Kogin, a variation of *sashiko*, is named after the *koginu*, a short jacket worn by farmers. Traditionally stitched on indigo fabric, the

Five-panel noren decorated with different geometric *sashiko* patterns inside in *giboshi* (welsh onion flower) motifs by Eiko Yoshida.

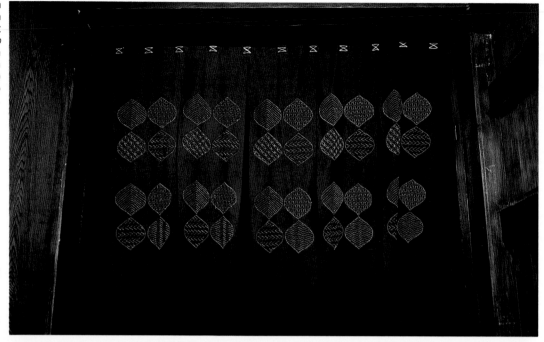

Cotton *zabuton* cushions with different traditional patterns by Eiko Yoshida are very inviting when placed around big old wooden *hibachi*.

Magnificent *asanoha* (hemp-leaf)-patterned kimono with a contemporary feeling. Needlework in different-color threads on indigo blue background by Eiko Yoshida.

running stitches of white thread in *kogin* are uneven in length and go only in the direction of the weft. Originally used on work clothes, these beautiful, densely stitched geometric designs now adorn jackets, purses, belts, shawls, and wall hangings.

A third variation of *sashiko*, *hitomezashi* (one stitch), requires only one stitch in any given direction to create its intricate geometric motifs. Its reversible designs transform potholders, vests, cushion covers, and tea accessories into vibrant utilitarian art works.

From drawing to actual needlework in *kogin*.

The top part of both jackets is stitched very densely, resembling fine lace.

Various patterns
are applied to
scarf, handbags,
shawls, belt, and
seal-case.

Geometric patterns beautifully designed for an obi by Setsu Maeda.

Ainu Textiles

Applique and Embroidery

The Sky People, as the Ainu call themselves, live in the snow country. Hokkaido, the Kuriles, and southern Sakhalin Island are their homes. Among their handicraft products, textiles are the most important. Though once numerous, Ainu craftsmen trained in the old techniques are disappearing, leaving behind only a few reminders of their textile heritage, now seen in museums and an occasional antique shop.

For ages, the Ainu have made and decorated their clothing and utensils according to ancient traditions. Textiles were the province of the Ainu women, while wood carving was that of the men. Before marriage, a courting couple exchanged gifts. For her, he made a carved knife; she wove and embroidered clothing for him. After marriage, to renew their vows, the husband made a knife sheath, a shuttle, and a loom as his gifts, and the wife reciprocated with items of clothing beautifully decorated with embroidery or applique.

The Ainu sometimes made clothing from animal and fish—in particular, salmon—skins, by sewing together and creating patchwork patterns of furs and skins in different colors and textures. But they also wove their own fabric, called *atsushi*, from the bark of elm trees. The bark, stripped from the trees, was soaked in water for from one week to ten days to soften it, then pulled apart to make threads. These threads were rolled into balls and saved to be woven later into cloth on a simple backstrap loom. Some of the fibers were put aside for sewing thread, which was made by the women who chewed the strings to make them soft.

The Ainu women used two methods to applique symmetrical traditional motifs onto

Aharushi, a large black traditional symmetric motif applied on bast-fiber cloth with embroidery.

Ruunpe, strips of fabrics in different c

124

already completed garments: *kirifuse*, or cutting and applying large designs, and *nuno oki*, or cutting and applying small designs. Then with heavy colored threads imported from the mainland of Japan, the Ainu women embroidered additional motifs, using the chain, stem, buttonhole, satin, and couching stitches.

The motifs were symmetrical, following the belief that their symmetry equally protected all parts of the wearer's body. Of the same importance was the placement of the designs. All openings, armholes, necklines, and hems, were decorated in order to keep evil spirits from entering the wearer's body through them. These simple but forceful motifs, in the form of spirals and thorns which resemble braces, are reminiscent of the motifs of the Jomon Period in Japan and the serpent motifs of ancient China. Ainu textile designs are unique and splendid in spite of their limited materials.

Pirikachikiriimi, beautifully embroidered in different colors.

textures appliqued symmetrically.

Kaparamibu, applique combined with embroidery.

6

Contemporary Creations

Hidden away in dark corners, brilliantly displayed on hanging racks, or folded neatly on shelves, beautiful textiles reveal themselves to the casual and the avid shopper alike. With their beauty and value in mind, resourceful people mull over ways in which to display these masterpieces. Some pieces have obvious functions–a wall hanging or a drape for the sofa–while others invite more thought for their display and require a great deal of ingenuity. We have included a few of the many ways in which antique, slightly used, and new textiles are put on display. We hope that this will stimulate interest in revitalizing the traditional textile crafts and techniques and that it will encourage people to find new ways of applying the traditions of old in modern creations.

Maureen Duxbury combined a solid purple kimono of the Showa era with a Taisho-era obi of a different shade of purple in a screen format.

126

Pretty flowers and grasses are delicately embroidered by Shizuka Kusano.

Naomi Hoff used old kimono to make a contemporary bedspread with striking color combinations.

A patchwork quilt made by Sunny Yang using various geometric and traditional Japanese designs from indigo-dyed cotton *yukata* fabrics.

In creating cushions, Shizuka Kusano used traditional techniques and motifs of Japanese embroidery, adding original designs to meet contemporary tastes and practical needs.

A two-panel folding screen by Maureen Duxbury with a Heian-period hunting scene from a formal kimono of the late Taisho era.

Blue-and-white *yukata* (cotton kimono) fabric is used for a fan-shaped placemat with matching napkins by Tomoyo Tsuchiya.

The basic techniques of Japanese embroidery displayed in a sampler by Sachiko Suzuki: *suganui* (autumn flowers and grasses), *sashinui* (peony), *nuikiri* (mum), *warinui* (leaves), *matsurinui* (outline of leaves), and *komanui* (couching).

To create sculpturelike wall-hangings Masako Hayashibe weaves with natural fibers dyed with natural dyes. Wire produces the dramatic three-dimensional effect.

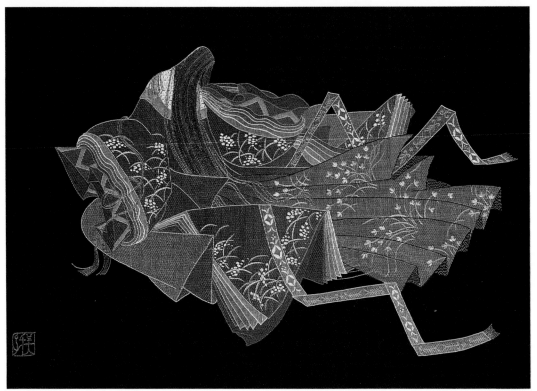

The wall decoration of *juni-hitoe* (twelve unlined robes) embroidered by Sachiko Suzuki.

The embroidery of
Seiji Ishikawa is
unique for its
woven appear-
ance. His wall
decoration is
embelished with
peonies.

The image of clouds and sky are beautifully expressed by Akiko Shimanuki using a primitive weaving technique, in which the warp threads between two bars are braided by fingers.

Yuya Nagahata uses kimono fabrics in richly colored Western-style dresses. His *rinzu* culottes display fluttering curved layers in subtle patterns.

The red silk crepe under-kimono of the Meiji era is recreated into elegant and exotic evening wear with a huge crane on the back. By Elke Oellerich.

This silk coat is striking in color with auspicious symbols from traditional kimono motifs by Yuya Nagahata.

A black satin jacket with a richly woven carp on the back is perfect for any occasion. By Elke Oellerich.

A cotton Ainu coat-dress that can be worn as an outer coat in breezy weather or alone on warmer days. By Oellerik.

This black silk jacket with red lining is roomy, comfortable, and exciting in a bright red design by Oellerik.

This expressive hat is created from obi fabrics by Antoinette Maclachlan.

Front and back of a half-coat made from an obi combined with obi padding. By Anne Lecut.

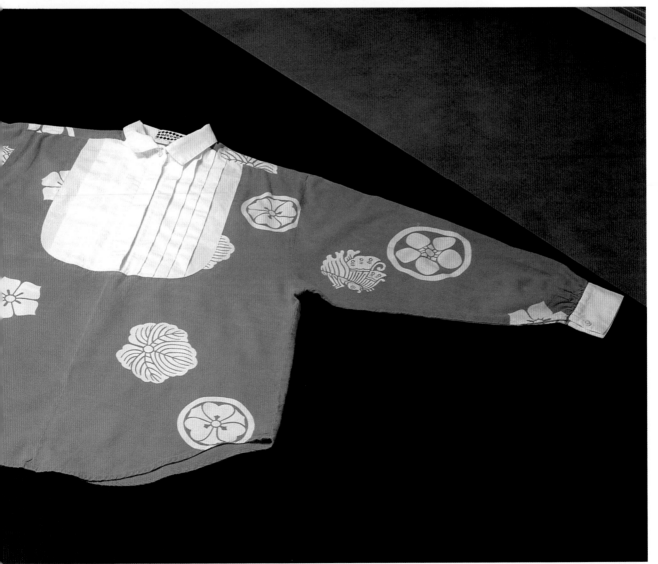

Carol Thurstons cotton blouse of blue and white *yukata* fabric combined with plain white is handsomely designed.

Kyoko Kanazawa's jacket is created by combining traditional *sashiko* techniques and motifs with her own modern designs.

Guyllemette Hausey-Leplat was fascinated by the *katazome* of the late Keisuke Serizawa at his exhibition in Paris. *City in the Foggy Rain*, the scenery of Shinjuku in contemporary *katazome*.

Museums and Galleries

The museums and galleries listed below all have textile collections worth seeing, and their other collections are often of great interest as well. Most museums in Japan are closed on Mondays and over the New Year holidays. Some are also closed for a period in the summer. Galleries also observe weekly and seasonal holidays. (It's always a good idea to check with the museum or gallery you plan to visit before you start out.) At museums, a modest entrance fee usually is charged. Special exhibitions are regularly announced in the Japanese and English-language press.

Tokyo and Its Vicinity

Bunka Fashion Museum (Bunka Gakuen Fukushoku Hakubutsukan). 3-22-1 Yoyogi, Shibuya-ku, Tokyo. Tel: (03) 299-2387. Fabrics, costumes, kimono, Noh costumes, and other Japanese, Western, and Asian fabrics and costumes. Seven-minute walk from the south exit of JR Shinjuku Station, on the Koshu Kaido.

Crafts Gallery, National Museum of Modern Art (Kogei Kan, Kokuritsu Kindai Bijutsukan). 1 Kitanomaru Koen, Chiyoda-ku, Tokyo. Tel: (03) 211-7781. Dyed textiles, porcelain, lacquerware, metal-work. Eight-minute walk from Tozai Line Takebashi Station, toward Hanzomon on Kinokuni Hill.

Eisei Bunko Museum (Eisei Bunko). 1-1-1, Mejirodai, Bunkyo-ku, Tokyo. Tel: (03) 941-0850. The notable collection of the Hosokawa family. Noh costumes, lacquerware, metal-work, armors. Fifteen-minute walk from Tozai Line Waseda Station.

Japan Folk Crafts Museum (Nippon Mingeikan). 4-3-33 Komaba, Meguro-ku, Tokyo. Tel: (03) 467-4527. Textiles, kimono, chests (*tansu*), screens, pottery. Near Inokashira Line Komaba Todai-mae Station.

Japan Traditional Craft Center (Zenkoku Dentoteki Kogeihin Senta). Plaza 246 Building, 2 Fl., 3-1-1 Minami Aoyama, Minato-ku, Tokyo. Tel: (03) 403-2460. Three-minute walk from the Ginza Subway Line Gaien-mae Station, on Aoyama-dori.

National Museum of Japanese History (Kokuritsu Rekishi Minzoku Hakubutsukan). 117 Jonai-cho, Sakura-shi, Chiba-ken. Tel: (0434) 86-0123. The Nomura Shojiro collection of kimono and textiles from the sixteenth through the nineteenth century, one of the finest in Japan, is here. It consists of 156 *kosode* robes and over 120 partial robes mounted on screens. Ten to fifteen-minute walk from the Keisei Line Keisei Sakura Station.

Silk Museum (Shiruku Hakubutsukan). 1 Yamashita-cho, Naka-ku, Yokohama. Tel: (045) 641-0841/0843. Original *kosode*, kimono, Noh costumes, reproductions of costumes, and dolls from the Edo through the Taisho period. Take a taxi or bus from Sakuragicho Station on either the JR Keihin Tohoku Line or the Toyoko Line.

Suntory Museum (Suntory Bijutsukan). Suntory Building, 1-2-3 Moto Akasaka, Minato-ku, Tokyo. Tel: (03) 470-1073. Important Japanese textiles. Five-minute walk from Ginza or Marunouchi Subway Line Akasakamitsuke Station.

Tokyo National Museum (Tokyo Kokuritsu Hakubutsukan). 13-9, Ueno Koen, Taito-ku, Tokyo. Tel: (03) 822-1111. Clothes worn by the nobility, the military, commoners, and costumes used in popular entertainments. Ten minute-walk from the west exit of the JR Yamanote Line Ueno Station.

Toyama Museum (Toyama Kinenkan). 675, Oaza Shironuma, Kawashima-machi, Hiki-gun, Saitama-ken. Tel: (0492) 97-0007. From folk textiles to *tsujigahana*, and examples of weaving and dyeing from India, Indonesia, Iran, and other countries. Take the Tobu Tojo Line to Kawagoe Station, and leave from the east exit. Take the Okegawa-yuki bus to Ushigayado bus station (about twenty to twenty-five minutes), or a taxi. Taxi fare is about two thousand yen.

Kyoto City

Kodai Yuzen'en with Yuzen Gallery (Yuzen Bijutsukan Kodai Yuzen'en). Inokuma Nishi-iru, Takatsuji-dori, Shimogyo-ku, Kyoto. Tel: (075) 811-8101. Traditional textiles and dyeing techniques. On Horikawa-dori.

Kyoto National Museum (Kyoto Kokuritsu Hakubutsukan). 527 Chaya-machi, Higashiyama-ku, Kyoto. Tel: (075) 541-1151. A major collection of dyed and woven fabrics. Ten-munute walk from

JR Kyoto Station.

Kyoto Prefectural General Museum (Kyoto Furitsu Sogo Shiryokan). 1-4 Hangi-cho, Shimogamo, Sakyo-ku, Kyoto. (075) 781-9101. Excellent examples of *tsujigahana* and other woven and dyed fabrics. Take the Midorogaike-yuki bus from JR Kyoto Station and get off at Sogo Shiryokan-mae.

Nishijin Textile Center (Nishijin Ori Kaikan). Imadegawa Minami-iru, Horikawa-dori, Kamigyo-yu, Kyoto. Tel: (075) 451-9231. Historical materials and kimono. Take a bus from JR Kyoto Station and get off at Horikawa/Imadegawa-dori.

Shozan Dyeing and Weaving Gallery / Shozan Dyeing and Weaving Studio (Shozan Senshoku Gallery / Shozan Senshoku Kogei Kan). 47 Kagamiishi-cho, Kinugasa, Kita-ku, Kyoto. Tel: (075) 491-5101. Part of a large park with a Japanese garden, textile gallery, and restaurants.

Other Areas

Arimatsu-Narumi Shibori Museum (Arimatsu Narumi Shibori Kaikan). 60-1 Hashi Higashi Minami, Arimatsu-cho, Midori-ku, Nagoya-shi, Aichi-ken. Tel: (052) 621-0111. More than one hundred traditional tie-dyeing patterns developed during the 370 years of the town's history. From JR Nagoya Station take the Meitetsu Nagoya Honsen train to Arimatsu (the express train does not stop there, so take or transfer to a local).

Hamakasuri Folk Arts Museum (Hamakasuri Mingeikan). 57 Oshinozu-cho, Yonago-shi, Tottori-ken. Tel: (0859) 25-1411. *Kasuri* from the San'in area. Take a Sotohama-Line bus bound for Sakai Minato from Yanago Station on the JR San'in Honsen Line. Get off at Watamisaki Jinja-mae.

Hayashibara Museum of Art (Hayashibara Bijutsukan). 2-7-15 Marunouchi, Okayama-shi, Okayama-ken. Tel: (0862)-23-1733. A superb collection of Noh costumes from the Momoyama period to the Edo period belonging to the Ikeda family. A few minutes by taxi from JR Okayama Station.

Hikone Castle Museum (Hikonejo Hakubutsukan). 1-1 Konki-machi, Hikone-shi, Shiga-ken. Tel: (0749) 22-5657. Possessions of the Ii family (feudal lord of Hikone) including Noh costumes and masks. About five minutes by taxi from JR Hikone Station.

Izumo Folk Arts Museum (Izumo Mingeikan). 628 Chiimiya-cho, Izumo-shi, Shimane-ken. Tel: (0853) 22-6397. *Tsutsugaki* collection. A five to seven-minute walk from Chiimiya Station on the JR San'in Honsen Line.

Matsumoto Folk Arts Museum (Matsumoto Mingeikan). 1313-1 Shimoganai, Satoyamabe, Matsumoto-shi, Nagano-ken. Tel: (0263) 33-1569. A good collection of *sashiko*. Take a Chuo-Line bus from JR Matsumoto Station bound for Utsukushi-gahara Onsen and get off at Shimoganai-mae.

Okinawa Prefectural Museum (Okinawa Kenritsu Hakubutsukan). 1-1 Onaka-machi, Shuri, Naha-shi, Okinawa-ken. Tel: (0988) 84-2234. A collection of about one thousand dyed and woven fabrics of Okinawa. Take a Sueyoshi-Line bus from Naha to Ikehata.

Shizuoka Municipal Serizawa Keisuke Museum (Shizuoka Shiritsu Serizawa Keisuke Bijutsukan). Toro Koen, 5-10-5 Toro, Shizuoka-shi, Shizuoka-ken. Tel: (0542) 82-5522. Renowned textile designer Keisuke Serizawa's textile collection, his varied designs, kimono, and noren. From the north exit of JR Shizuoka Station, take bus number four to Toro Tseki, the last stop.

Tokugawa Art Museum (Tokugawa Bijutsukan). 1017 Tokugawa-cho, Higashi-ku, Nagoya-shi, Aichi-ken. Tel: (052)935-6262. The finest Noh robes and masks in Japan. Also two quilted *kosode* worn by Ieyasu. From Nagoya City Bus Terminal, Green Platform number 7, take the bus for Jiyugaoka and get off at Shindeki.

Yukara Ori Folk Craft Museum (Yukara Ori Kogeikan). 37-218 Kamui-cho, Chuwa, Asahikawa-shi, Hokkaido. Tel: (0166) 62-8811. The colorful fabric designs of the Ainu textiles on display here reflect natural features of the northern region. About fifteen minutes from JR Asahikawa Station.

Bibliography

Adachi, Barbara. *The Living Treasures of Japan*. Tokyo and New York: Kodansha International, 1973.

Batchelor, John. *Ainu Life and Lore: Echoes of a Departing Race*. Tokyo: Kyobunkan, 1971.

Blakemore, Frances. *Japanese Design Through Textile Patterns*. New York and Tokyo: Weatherhill, 1978.

Brandon, Reiko Mochinaga. *Country Textiles of Japan: The Art of Tsutsugaki*. New York and Tokyo: Weatherhill, 1986.

Burnham, Dorothy K. *Warp and Weft: A Textile Terminology*. Toronto, Ontario: Royal Ontario Museum, 1980.

Dower, John W. *The Elements of Japanese Design: A Handbook of Family Crests, Heraldry, and Symbolism*. New York and Tokyo: Weatherhill, 1971.

Fontein, Jan, general editor. *Living National Treasures of Japan*. With contributions by Hiroshi Harada, Kunio Minami, Tetsuro Kitamura, Shin Yagihashi, Mikio Otaki, and Morihiro Ogawa. Translated by Patricia Massy, Shigetaka Kaneko, and Takehiro Shindo. Boston: The Museum of Fine Arts, 1983.

Gunsaulus, Helen. *Japanese Textiles*. New York: The Japan Society, 1941.

Hara, Reiko, Kazuko Saito, and Hiroko Nagai. *Japanese Paper Stencil Designs*. Tokyo: Hachiro Yuasa Memorial Museum, International Christian University, 1985.

Hauge, Victor and Takako. *Folk Traditions in Japanese Art*. Tokyo and New York: Kodansha International, 1978.

Hayashi, Ryoichi. *The Silk Road and the Shoso-in*. Translated by Robert Ricketts. The Heibonsha Survey of Japanese Art, vol. 6. New York and Tokyo: Weatherhill-Heibonsha, 1975.

Hirai, Noriko, editor. *Tsutsugaki Textiles of Japan*. Kyoto: Shikosha, 1987.

Ito, Toshiko. *Tsujigahana: The Flower of Japanese Textile Art*. Translated by Monica Bethe. Tokyo and New York: Kodansha International, 1981.

Japan Textile Color Design Center, The, comp. *Textile Designs of Japan*, revised edition, 3 vols: *Okinawa, Ainu, and Foreign Designs*. Tokyo and New York: Kodansha International, 1980.

Kaemmerer, Eric A. *Trades and Crafts of Old Japan*. Rutland, Vermont and Tokyo: Charles E. Tuttle Co., 1961.

Kidder, J. E. Jr., Reiko Hara, Akiko Fukuno, and Kazuko Saito. *Japanese Indigo Textiles*. Tokyo: Hachiro Yuasa Memorial Museum, International Christian University, 1987.

Kirihata, Ken. *Kyogen Costumes*. London: Thames and Hudson, 1980.

Lee, Sherman E. *The Genius of Japanese Design*. Tokyo and New York: Kodansha International, 1981.

Matsumoto, Kaneo. *Jodai Gire: 7th and 8th Century Textiles in Japan from the Shoso-in and Horyu-ji*. Translated by Shigetaka Kaneko and Richard L. Mellott. Tokyo: Shikosha, 1984.

Meech-Pekarik, Julia. *Momoyama: Japanese Art in the Age of Grandeur*. New York: The Metropolitan Museum of Art, 1975.

Minnich, Helen Benton, with Shojiro Nomura. *Japanese Costume and the Makers of Its Elegant Tradition*. Rutland, Vermont and Tokyo: Charles E. Tuttle Co., 1963.

Mizoguchi, Saburo. *Design Motifs*. Translated by Louise Allison Cort. Arts of Japan, vol. 1. New York and Tokyo: Weatherhill-Shibundo, 1973.

Moes, Robert. *Mingei: Japanese Folk Art. From the Brooklyn Museum Collection*. Ainu section by Anne Pike Tay. New York: Universe Books, 1985.

Morita, Kimio. *Embroidery*. Nihon no Bijutsu

(Japanese art), vol. 59. Tokyo: Shibundo, 1981.

Munsterberg, Hugo. *The Folk Arts of Japan*. Rutland, Vermont and Tokyo: Charles E. Tuttle Co., 1958.

Muraoka, Kageo, and Kichiemon Okamura. *Folk Arts and Crafts of Japan*. Translated by Daphne D. Stegmaier. The Heibonsha Survey of Japanese Art, vol. 26. New York and Tokyo: Weatherhill-Heibonsha, 1973.

Nakano, Eisha and Barbara B. Stephan. *Japanese Stencil Dyeing: Paste-Resist Techniques*. New York and Tokyo: Weatherhill, 1982.

The National Museum of Modern Art, Kyoto. *Craft Treasures of Okinawa*. With contributions by Michiaki Kawakita, Seiko Hokama, Yoshinobu Tokugawa, Hirokazu Arakawa, and Yoshitaro Kamakura. Tokyo and New York: Kodansha International, 1978.

Noma, Seiroku. *Japanese Costume and Textile Arts*. Translated by Armins Nikovskis. The Heibonsha Survey of Japanese Art, vol. 16. New York and Tokyo: Weatherhill-Heibonsha, 1974.

Saint-Gilles, Amaury. *Mingei: Japan's Enduring Folk Art*. Tokyo: Fuji Bijutsu Insatsu Co. Ltd., 1983.

Saito, Rei. *Sashiko Zukushi* (All about *sashiko*). Tokyo: Bunka Shuppankyoku, 1986.

Yamazaki, Seiju. *Kusakizome: Nihon no Iro Hyakunijusshoku* (Natural dyes, 120 colors). Tokyo: Bijutsu Shuppansha, 1982.

Stanley-Baker, Joan. *Japanese Art*. London: Thames and Hudson, 1984.

Stinchecum, Amanda Mayer. *Kosode: 16th—19th Century Textiles from the Nomura Collection*. Essays by Monica Bethe and Margot Paul. Tokyo and New York: Japan Society and Kodansha International, 1984.

Sugihara, Nobuhiko, and Hayao Ishimura, Mitsuhiko Hasebe, Masami Shiraishi, and Toyojiro

Hida. *Katazome: Japanese Stencil and Print Dyeing*. Tokyo: The National Museum of Modern Art, 1980.

Suzuki, Hisao. *Living Crafts of Okinawa*. New York and Tokyo: Weatherhill, 1973.

Tokugawa, Yoshinobu. *The Tokugawa Collection: Noh Robes and Masks*. Japan House Gallery, Japan Society, New York, 1977.

Tokugawa Art Museum, The. *The Shogun Age Exhibition*. Tokyo: Shogun no Jidai-ten Jimukyoku, 1983.

Tomita, Jun and Noriko. *Japanese Ikat Weaving: The Techniques of Kasuri*. London, Boston, Melbourne, and Henley: Rutledge and Kegan Paul, Ltd., 1982.

Wada, Yoshiko, Mary Kellogg Rice, and Jane Barton. *Shibori: The Inventive Art of Japanese Shaped Resist Dyeing*. Tokyo and New York: Kodansha International, 1983.

Yamanaka, Norio. *The Book of Kimono*. Tokyo and New York: Kodansha International, 1982.

Yamanobe, Tomoyuki, *Noh Costumes and Robes*. Tokyo: The Okura Shukokan Museum, 1977.

Yamanobe, Tomoyuki. *Opulence: The Kimonos and Robes of Itchiku Kubota*. Tokyo and New York: Kodansha International, 1984.

Yanagi, Soetsu. *The Unknown Craftsman: A Japanese Insight Into Beauty*. Tokyo and New York: Kodansha International, 1972.

Yoshida, Eiko. *Sashiko Hyakuyo* (One hundred *sashiko* patterns). Tokyo: Bunka Shuppankyoku, 1986.

Yoshida, Mitsukuni. *Kire: Nihon no Some to Ori* (Fabric: Japanese dyeing and weaving). Tokyo: Shufunotomo, 1982.

Yoshikawa, Itsuji. *Major Themes in Japanese Art*. Translated by Armins Nikovskis. The Heibonsha Survey of Japanese Art, vol. 1. New York and Tokyo: Weatherhill-Heibonsha, 1976.

Sources

50cm-No-Kimono
(Kimono fabric sold from 50cm)
Gallery Court Heim 1F
4-5-17, Motoyama Naka-machi
Higashi Nada-ku, Kobe-shi
Hyogo Pref. 658
Tel: (078) 413-0050

Akariya Antiques
(Antique kimono and obi)
4-8-1, Yoyogi
Shibuya-ku, Tokyo 151
Tel: (03) 465-5578

Blue & White (Yukata fabrics)
2-9-2, Azabu Juban
Minato-ku, Tokyo 106
Tel: (03) 451-0537

Duxbury, Maureen
(Screen designer)
1-10-19, Hatanodai
Shinagawa-ku, Tokyo 142
Tel: (03) 787-9860
         and
1710 Purdue Avenue #303
West Los Angeles
Calif. 90025, U.S.A.
Tel: (213) 473-1718

Hausey-Leplat, Guyllemette
(Katazome)
6-29-72-6, Sagami Ono
Sagamihara-shi,
Kanagawa Pref. 228
Tel: (0427) 48-5376

Hayashibe, Masako (Weaver)
M & Y Fine Selected Co.
1-2-9, Jingumae
Shibuya-ku, Tokyo 150
Tel: (03) 405-7870

Hoff, Naomi (Designer)
Nami, Shiba Shirogane Hills #203
5-12-3, Shiroganedai
Minato-ku, Tokyo 108
Tel: (03) 444-9263

Japan Traditional Craft Center
Plaza 246 Building
3-1-1, Minami Aoyama

Minato-ku, Tokyo 107
Tel: (03) 403-2468

Kanazawa, Kyoko *(Sashiko)*
3-22-17, Asahi-cho
Kawagoe-shi, Saitama Pref. 350
Tel: (0492) 43-7460

Komada, Sakuko *(Katazome)*
Textile Design
1-10-8, Shoto
Shibuya-ku, Tokyo 150
Tel: (03) 467-8035

Kubo, Eisen *(Yuzen)*
2-22-7, Nakazato
Kita-ku, Tokyo 104
Tel: (03) 940-3428

Kubota, Itchiku *(Tsujigahana)*
Itchiku Tsujigahana
Seibu Department Store
2-5-1, Yurakucho
Chiyoda-ku, Tokyo 102
Tel: (03) 286-0111

Kusano, Shizuka
(Embroiderer)
1-11-34, Nakahara
Mitaka-shi, Tokyo 181
Tel: (03) 300-7656

Lecut, Anne (Designer)
399 Renkoji, Tama-shi
Tokyo 192-02
Tel: (0423) 76-8174

Maclachlan, Antoinette
(Milliner designer)
San-ei-so Sugamachi 8
Shinjuku-ku, Tokyo 160
Tel: (03) 357-6248

Matsumoto, Midori
(Fashion designer)
Midori International Co., Ltd.
3-51-10 Sendagaya
Shibuya-ku, Tokyo 151
Tel: (03) 470-6525

Moriguchi, Kako *(Yuzen)*
Mitsukoshi Department Store

1-4, Nihombashi Muromachi
Chuo-ku, Tokyo 103
Tel: (03) 241-3311

Nagahata, Yuya
(Fashion designer)
Boutique Yuya
3-6-4, Nishi-azabu
Minato-ku, Tokyo 106
Tel: (03) 5474-2097

Nishikawa (Antique kimono)
2-20-14, Azabu-juban
Minato-ku, Tokyo 106
Tel: (03) 456-1023

Oellerich, Elke (Designer)
Talweg 1, 8011 Kirchseeon
West Germany
Tel: 08091-2314

Omoshiroya (Antiques)
1-10-21-101, Kichijoji Higashi-cho
Musashino-shi, Tokyo 180
Tel: (0422) 22-8565

Oriental Bazaar (Antiques)
5-9-13, Jingumae
Shibuya-ku, Tokyo 150
Tel: (03) 400-3933

Suzuki, Sachiko (Embroiderer)
Nui, 3-4-9, Azabudai
Minato-ku, Tokyo 106
Tel: (03) 405-7850

Tokyo Antique Hall
2-9, Kanda Surugadai
Chiyoda-ku, Tokyo 101
Tel: (03) 295-7112

Tsuchiya, Tomoyo (Designer)
Boutique Tomoyo
Gody Building 1F
6-8-8, Roppongi
Minato-ku, Tokyo 106
Tel: (03) 479-1176

Contemporary and antique
textiles can be obtained at major
department stores and antique
flea markets.

Index

Japanese Historical Periods

Jomon (Neolithic):
ca. 10,000–ca. 200 B.C.

Yayoi: ca. 200 B.C.–ca. A.D. 200

Kofun (Tumulus):
200–mid sixth century

Asuka: Late sixth century to 710

Nara: 710–794

Heian (Fujiwara): 794–1185

Kamakura: 1185–1333

Muromachi (Ashikaga): 1333–1568

Momoyama: 1568–1600

Edo (Tokugawa): 1600–1868

Meiji: 1868–1912

Taisho: 1912–26

Showa: 1926–89

Heisei: 1989–present

Photo Credit

Front cover: Antique textiles and a sewing box courtesy of Tokyo Antique Hall.
Title page: Section of a *kara ori* kimono with a pattern of waves and folding fans. Edo period. Tokyo National Museum.
P.11 Folding screen depicting a *komon* stencil dyer at work, a woman dyeing with indigo, and another dyed fabric drying. Late sixteenth century. Kitain Collection.
P.19 Section of *maru obi* with various fan motifs. Meiji period.

Tokyo National Museum.
P.46 Photograph by Noritoyo Nakamoto.
P.77 Using a fingernail and shuttle in weaving *tsuzure ori*. Photograph courtesy of Sekai Bunka Photo.
P.78 Noh photograph by Tadayuki Naito.
P.87 Saga *nishiki* handbag and *zori* courtesy of Mitsukoshi Department Store, Nihombashi, Tokyo.
P.109 Kabuki photograph by Yutaka Umemura.
P.119-121 Photographs by Akira

Tabuchi from the book, *Sashiko Hyakuyo*, by Eiko Yoshida. See bibliography.
P.124-125 Photographs of her Ainu textile collection courtesy of Mari Kodama.
P. 136 Photograph by Satomi Ono.
Back cover: Section of a *kara ori* Noh costume with chrysanthemum motifs. Ocean wave pattern in the background depicted with gold leaf. Edo period. Eisei Bunko collection.